Lighthouses of Atlantic Canada

New Brunswick, Nova Scotia, Prince Edward Island,
Newfoundland & Labrador

West Point Light, Prince Edward Island

Lighthouses of Atlantic Canada

New Brunswick, Nova Scotia, Prince Edward Island, Newfoundland & Labrador

A Pictorial Guide

Courtney Thompson

Designed, edited and published by
CatNap Publications
Mt. Desert, Maine

ISBN: 0-9651786-7-6
Library of Congress Catalog Card Number: **99-96228**

Photography, text, maps: Courtney Thompson

Cover photograph: Chris Mills

Additional photographs:
Chris Mills, pp.16, 17, 21, 22-23, 40, 43, 44-45, 47, 48-50, 54, 56, 57,
60-63, 64, 65, 78, 79, 81, 82, 92, 93, 94, 95, 100, 102 103,107, 108

Wanda Barrett, pp.112, 115, 116

Printed in Canada by
Quebecor Atlantic
St. John, New Brunswick
Canada

For purchase information please contact:
CatNap Publications
P.O. Box 848
Mt. Desert, ME. 04660
(207) 244-0485

For my father. His forethought and love made this project possible

Table of Contents

Nova Scotia

Shores of the Evangeline Trail & Lighthouse Route

Shores of the Evangeline Trail & Lighthouse Route (con't)

Northern & Eastern Shores, Halifax Area

Cape Breton Shores

Cape Breton Shores(con't)

Prince Edward Island

Western Shores-- West Point to North Cape

Central Shores --Charlottetown to Cavendish

Eastern Shores --Point Prim to East Point

Eastern Shores--Point Prim to East Point(con't)

Newfoundland & Labrador

Introduction

The provinces of Atlantic Canada are now rediscovering their lighthouses. Until recently, with continued progressive decommissioning by the Coast Guard, little thought was given to the valuable asset these structures represent. As a significant element of the maritime history and tradition of Atlantic Canada, the lighthouses are now seeing a gradual renaissance; they are being preserved rather than destroyed, restored rather than ignored, reconfigured as tourist sites and interpretive centers rather than abandoned to slow destruction by harsh weather, encroaching seas or intentional lack of care.

Foremost among the Atlantic provinces in lighthouse preservation, Nova Scotia has set the tone for this process. The Nova Scotia Lighthouse Preservation Society has become a vital, energetic, wide-ranging organization which took the lead in bringing lighthouses back from the verge of obscurity in Atlantic Canada. Today the group offers an interpretive center, offshore excursions, a regular publication and resource library; that Nova Scotia is readily associated with lighthouses is due in large part to the efforts of this group. Most recently Prince Edward Island has undertaken renovation and restoration of several lighthouses and has begun active promotion of those sites. The provinces of New Brunswick and Newfoundland have only recently begun to focus attention on their lighthouses as valuable resources, with a fledgling lighthouse preservation effort recently underway in Newfoundland.

Gathering information and images for this book therefore presented a particular challenge. The intent was not to include every lighthouse in each province, but rather to offer a comprehensive overview of each. Both Nova Scotia and Newfoundland have many offshore lighthouses which are at best difficult to access, oftentimes impossible. Additionally the remote, rugged coastline of Newfoundland presented a unique challenge. The directions are not uniformly specific but will, in all cases, offer a solid start; particularly in Newfoundland it's often necessary to ask local residents for assistance. The maps, likewise, are intended as an informal guide; in several instances specific lighthouses are noted in red when a map is repeated in succeeding layouts.

Particular contributions to this project require individual acknowledgment. Chris Mills was a lightkeeper in New Brunswick, Nova Scotia and British Columbia. During this tenure he was able to photograph a variety of lighthouses from a "first hand" perspective. A selection of those images enabled me to present unique views of several lighthouses; other images from his extensive collection added scope and dimension to the photographic presentations. The quality of his work represents a significant contribution to this book. Moreover, Chris was generous with his time and careful editorial comments. He continues to work actively with the Nova Scotia Lighthouse Preservation Society and readily offers his time in a variety of lighthouse venues.

Additionally, Wanda Barrett contributed images of particular Newfoundland lights, thereby enabling a more complete presentation of that section. Through her efforts, the beginnings of a lighthouse preservation society have been undertaken in that province. Finally, Ted and Jo Panayotoff again offered valuable editorial assistance, generously giving their time, input and friendship.

To all others who helped me along the way, in whatever manner, I extend my thanks and gratitude.

Atlantic Canada's Lighthouse Tradition

*M*ariners have navigated the waters of the North Atlantic for the past 500 years, but until the mid 18th century there were no lighthouses to guide them. Early on, after the first Europeans landed in Atlantic Canada, transport of goods and resources was dependent on safe passage and return of ships through the dangerous Canadian coastline. Lighthouses served to warn mariners away from possible shipwreck and to guide vessels carrying immigrants to Canada into safe harbors; they have now become representative of the nations maritime heritage.

Nova Scotia & New Brunswick

*T*he first Canadian lighthouse was built by the French in 1731 at Louisburg, Nova Scotia to guide military vessels into the harbor; it was not lit until 1734. That structure was destroyed by fire in 1736 but was quickly rebuilt of stone and bronze, the first fireproof building in North America. However, two years later the tower was destroyed by British cannon blast when the fortress was taken; it was not immediately rebuilt. The colonial government built a tower of similar "old world design" in 1758 on Sambro Island, Nova Scotia. Lit in 1759-60, this light has been in operation without interruption since that time, making it the oldest continuously operational lighthouse in North America.

New Brunswick's earliest recorded lighthouse was at Partridge Island on the Bay of Fundy, at the entrance to St. John Harbor. Loyalists first landed here May 10, 1783; the first immigration station in Canada was established on the island in 1784 and the light on Partridge Island was first lit in 1791. There developed a running feud between those who wanted lighthouses built to protect shipping interests and those who thought ships would be attracted by the lights and drawn onto the sand shoals and mudbanks. By 1832 even an official report noted that the New Brunswick Lighthouse Commissioners were so well content with the Bay of Fundy lights that an increase in number of lighthouses would "tend to perplex and embarrass the mariner on his voyage from seaward."

However, when loyalists came to New Brunswick by sea after the war of 1776 they were often landed back in their port of origination due to lack of navigational aids. Enough complaints, particularly by shipping interests, prompted a final reversal of this position, leading to the construction of more lights. Construction and maintenance were paid for by levying taxes. The Bay of Fundy, the great vein of water between the provinces of New Brunswick and Nova Scotia, boasting particularly unreliable waters, notorious fog and up to 54-foot tides is now one of the best lit areas on the east coast.

Newfoundland & Labrador

*L*ighthouses of Newfoundland and Labrador were built on some of the wildest and most magnificent capes and headlands of the world. Early in the 19th century these lights were navigational aids for trans-Atlantic mariners and local fishermen. Ancestors of today's Newfoundlanders were fishermen who stayed on the island when the fishing fleets returned to England. At that time, colonization was banned and Newfoundland recognized only as a temporary shelter for the cod fishing fleets. Sperm whale oil also developed into a source of revenue for those who fished the waters off Newfoundland, replacing candles and mineral oils for lighting London ballrooms. The first light on the island was built in 1813 at Ft. Amherst atop a stone fortress at the mouth of St. John's Harbor; 20 years would pass before another lighthouse was built along the Newfoundland coast. Today there remain 24 staffed stations in Newfoundland, matched only by British Columbia.

Prince Edward Island

*R*elatively sheltered from the Atlantic by Nova Scotia and Newfoundland, Prince Edward Island remains fairly free of fog. Shipbuilding and fishing were primary industries of the initial settlements; lighthouses were essential to navigation during the island's shipping and shipbuilding boom in mid-nineteenth century. The first lighthouse on PEI was built at Point Prim in 1846 and is one of only a few round, brick lighthouses in Canada. Typically, lighthouses on the island fall into two basic categories in terms of structure: (1) a freestanding tower, usually octagonal although square towers were the norm after PEI joined the Confederation in 1873, (2) a tower attached to a dwelling unit, typically a simple one storey, gable-roofed structure. PEI lights, as in Atlantic Canada in general, were primarily built of timber frame construction due to the abundance of wood with Point Prim being the notable exception.

Smaller range and harbor lights were built as utilitarian skeletons of iron, steel or wood. Although these small lights on jetties, piers and harbor entrances lack the glamour and glory of great coastal navigation and landfall lighthouses, they have an importance disproportionate to their size. Most shipwrecks occur near land; ships and mariners more readily handle the perils of the sea than hazards of an unmarked reef or rock, harbor arm or jetty. The first lighthouses built around the shores of Europe were guiding lights intended only to lead mariners the last mile or so to port; the many small harbor lights of Prince Edward Island do just that. Electrification was not entirely brought to PEI lighthouses until the 1950s; conversion to mercury vapor lamps followed in the 1970s.

Construction & Design

*I*nitially Canadian lighthouses were built of stone and mortar in the European manner; octagonal stone towers were standard construction during the 18th and early 19th centuries. This design was first adopted for the tower at Sambro Island. However, wood construction became the norm throughout the 19th century, using the same design as the stone structures. Factors responsible for this change in material were: lower building costs, abundance of local timber, shorter construction time and ready supply of skilled carpenters capable of erecting sturdy wooden structures. Cedar shingles were the primary exterior for the Atlantic towers because they resisted rot, an important quality in the damp climate. Despite predictions that the wooden towers would not withstand the elements as those of stone construction, the lighthouses fared well. By 1790 Nova Scotia had four lighthouses; by 1820 there were 10. The number of lights along the Atlantic Canada coast increased gradually during the next 15 years. The shipbuilding boom in Canada's Atlantic provinces prompted a flurry of lighthouse construction starting in 1829 with Head Harbour on Campobello Island (NB). By 1835 there were ten lights in the Bay of Fundy and eight on the Atlantic Coast. Newfoundland had one lighthouse.

During the years 1857-60 an ambitious three-year building program was undertaken whereby all materials and construction costs were borne by Great Britain. These lighthouses were designated "Imperial Lights" and, for the most part, were tall conical towers of brick or masonry construction. In some cases the granite was quarried and prepared by Scottish stonemasons and shipped to the colony as ballast. By the time Canada was formed (1867), Nova Scotia had 53 lights. Following Confederation, another period of lighthouse construction occurred. During the 1870s more than 100 new lighthouses went into operation. A large number were tapering wooden towers, usually four or eight sided. These structures were inexpensive to build and could be relatively easily relocated if erosion threatened the site (Miscou Is., and Mulholland in New Brunswick, Panmure Is., East Point, North Cape, West Point and Wood Islands in PEI, Margaretsville, NS). Additionally, many towers built during the 1870-1900 period were attached to the dwelling; a significant number of harbor and range lights also were constructed.

The chairman of the Lighthouse Board planned an extensive program of construction and upgrading during 1900-1914. Fresnel lenses were installed and numerous wooden towers were replaced with reinforced concrete or cast iron. From 1910-1950 the reinforced concrete tower began to replace the octagonal pattern; this provided, at low cost, an unlimited range of forms with strength and durability which could be readily upgraded without replacement.

The Lightkeepers

Canadian lightkeepers have served on some of the most isolated outposts, through some of the fiercest winters recorded in the world. Today there are 52 staffed lightstations in all Canada; at the turn of the century there were approximately 800. The first keepers were without shelter of even the tower and had to keep open fires going throughout the night in order to mark the edge of a rocky cliff or dangerous waterway in order to guide mariners to safe landfall. In the early 1800s, keepers focused primarily on making certain the light burned without interruption, cleaning the accumulation of soot from the lantern room and trimming the wick. More duties were added by mid 19th century as fog horns were added to lightstations. These fog alarm systems varied but most were bells, whistles or sirens; later powerful and efficient diaphones were typically used. One keeper, however, reportedly employed a set of old church bells and another a series of drums.

Living conditions in many cases were drafty, damp dwellings and the hours long. An 1875 Marine and Fisheries publication described instruction to lighthouse keepers, noting that care of the lens included " daily, patient and skillful application of manual labor in rubbing their surfaces", adding that any scratches or stains on the lens surfaces must be "due to dust and careless work". Each reflector had to be cleaned twice daily; the lens was to be dismantled and polished twice weekly.

Weather could be a treacherous element to contend with, particularly fog. A keeper on Machias Seal Island once waited three weeks on the mainland while his wife tended the light because thick fog prevented his return.

Equipment

Argand lamps and parabolic reflectors, developed in the early 1780s, were widely used in Canada until the late 19th century. Copper sheets were formed into a parabolic curve and plated with silver; the highly polished plates concentrated light rays into a horizontal beam, but about 50% of the light was lost. In the late 1700s Augustin Fresnel developed an improved refracting system. The Fresnel lens made use of a central lamp surrounded by lenses set into a metal frame and incorporated both reflection and refraction. Concentric rings of glass were placed one above the other horizontally to the light source; light rays moving vertically were reflected, concentrated and projected horizontally. With this system only about 10% of the light was lost. The lamps burned whale or seal oil until the 1850s but, by the mid 1860s, had been converted to coal oil or kerosene for economic and technical reasons. Kerosene was invented by a Nova Scotian, Abraham Gesner, and first tested at Maugher's Beach lighthouse in the late 1840s. In the early 1900s petroleum vapor lamps increased candlepower by more than 300%; many lights were converted to acetylene gas lamps. By the 1930s, some lights and rotational machinery were powered by electricity.

Lighthouses were identifiable not only by the color and characteristic of the light, but also by distinguishing marks. On the seaward side many had horizontal red bands, vertical stripes or black squares. These day markers were intended to make the structure more visible, especially when winter snow made the white building blend into the landscape.

Automated equipment was making manned lightstations obsolete by the 1960s. Between 1970 and 1986, 264 lighthouses in Canada were automated. Only 52 stations still are staffed, with 25 in Atlantic Canada (24 in Newfoundland, one in New Brunswick). Destaffing has been halted for the present. A few structures no longer needed for navigational purposes were transferred to local authorities, private groups or Parks Canada; surplus structures are now often offered for sale. Throughout Atlantic Canada efforts gradually are being undertaken to save and restore the lighthouse as significant element of cultural heritage and to preserve the spirit of the lightkeeping tradition, a vital part of Canada's maritime history.

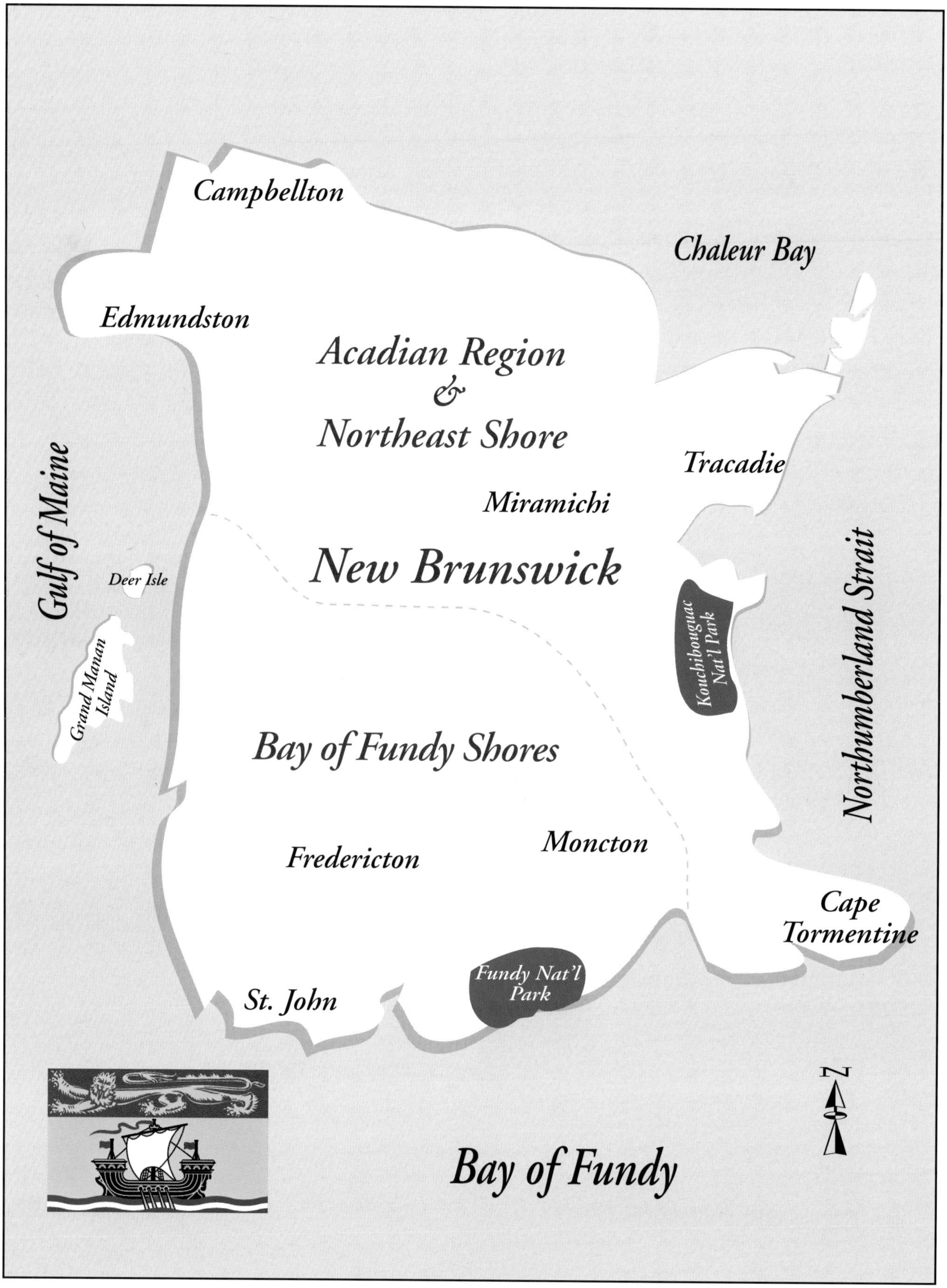

Campbellton

Chaleur Bay

Edmundston

Acadian Region
&
Northeast Shore

Tracadie

Gulf of Maine

Miramichi

New Brunswick

Deer Isle

Kouchibouguac Nat'l Park

Northumberland Strait

Grand Manan Island

Bay of Fundy Shores

Fredericton

Moncton

Cape Tormentine

Fundy Nat'l Park

St. John

N

Bay of Fundy

Bay of Fundy Shores
Campobello Island to Cape Enrage

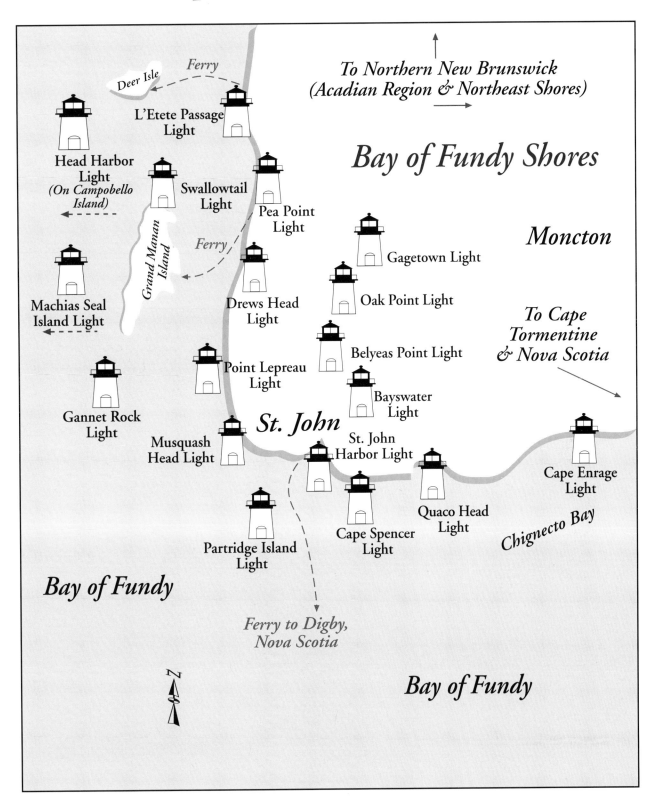

Ferry

Deer Isle

L'Etete Passage Light

Head Harbor Light
(On Campobello Island)

Swallowtail Light

Pea Point Light

To Northern New Brunswick (Acadian Region & Northeast Shores)

Bay of Fundy Shores

Moncton

Gagetown Light

Grand Manan Island

Ferry

Oak Point Light

Drews Head Light

Machias Seal Island Light

Belyeas Point Light

To Cape Tormentine & Nova Scotia

Point Lepreau Light

Bayswater Light

Gannet Rock Light

St. John

Musquash Head Light

St. John Harbor Light

Cape Enrage Light

Quaco Head Light

Chignecto Bay

Partridge Island Light

Cape Spencer Light

Bay of Fundy

Ferry to Digby, Nova Scotia

N

Bay of Fundy

Twelve miles off the coast from Cutler, Maine, this light station is maintained by the Canadian government although it is in waters claimed both by the United States and Canada. Canadian lightkeepers man the station due to a question of sovereignty, with both Canada and the United States claiming the island and surrounding waters. The island is home to a large puffin colony and other sea birds, carefully protected by the Canadian Wildlife Service. Charter trips to view the light and the puffins are available from Grand Manan Is., Jonesport and Cutler, Maine.

Machias Seal Island Light

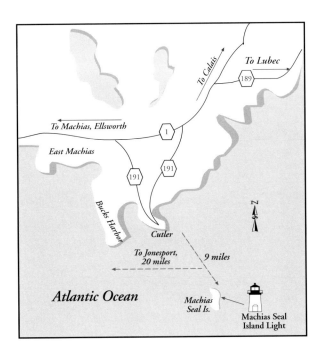

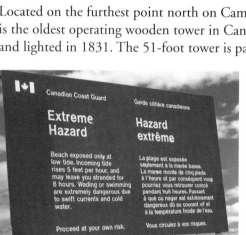

East Quoddy Head Light

Located on the furthest point north on Campobello Island, the light is the oldest operating wooden tower in Canada, built in 1829-30 and lighted in 1831. The 51-foot tower is painted with the cross of St. George; the distinctive daymark has been on the structure at least since Confederation.

Alexander Findlay in 1867 wrote that "the lighthouses of New Brunswick and Nova Scotia, where necessary, are painted with black or red stripes to distinguish the towers from the land." He continues, "after the snow is gone off the land, the accumulations against the fences, which generally run at right angles to the coast, and which continue for some time after it (the snow) has disappeared from the fields themselves, have exactly the appearance of a white tower." The light is also known as Head Harbour Light.

During the 1820s trade flourished and traffic increased between Campobello and the Maine coast. Fog, high tides and treacherous rocks around the island cut into profits of sea-faring traders. The lighthouse was the first Canadian response to these dangers, built to warn mariners of the craggy rocks and shoals in the area.

In the final years leading to destaffing of the station in 1986, the assistant keeper lived in the attached keeper's dwelling, while the principal keeper lived "ashore" on Campobello, just at the end of the road leading to the lighthouse.

Summer home of Franklin Roosevelt, Campobello Island, NB-en route to East Quoddy Lighthouse

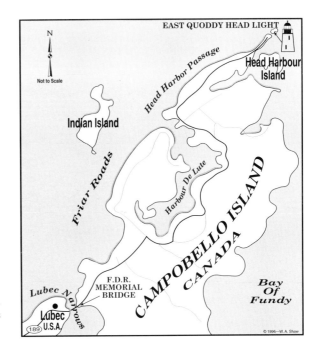

Directions: Cross into Campobello, Is. at Lubec, Maine and continue approximately 2.5 miles past the customs station and Roosevelt Park. Turn right at a"Y" intersection, NB 774 North. Continue on this road for about seven miles through Wilson's Beach to Head Harbour and the light. The road (Lighthouse Rd) becomes a dirt road shortly before ending at the parking area. (Or take the ferry from Deer Isle, New Brunswick)

There are trails around the area, including series of iron rail stairways which make the light accessible directly at low tide only. A sign warns of rapidly changing tides and weather conditions; there is about a two-hour period to cross and return from the light without being stranded on the island for six to eight hours.

Mulholland Light

On the east side of Lubec Channel on Campobello Island, the light is easily seen from the Maine side of the channel and is easily accessible from the Canadian side. The lighthouse is part of the Roosevelt Campobello International Park and picnic grounds. Mulholland is not a functioning light.

*"Mulholland Point Lighthouse
Erected 1885
Donated to
Roosevelt Campobello International Park
December 4, 1985"*

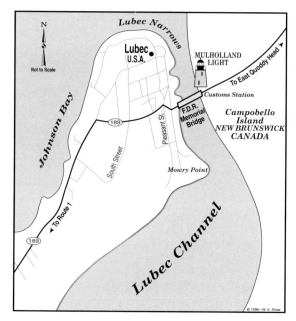

Directions: Cross over to New Brunswick, Canada at Lubec, Maine, taking the first left after the customs station, just opposite the welcome/information center. The road leads down a hill, then bears right; a small park and the light are just to the left.

Swallowtail Light

The first visitors to Grand Manan Island may have been Passamaquoddy Indians, followed in 1606 by explorer Samuel de Champlain who added the word "Grand" to "Manan", a corruption of the original Indian name meaning "island in the sea". The island subsequently changed hands several times, according to the results of wars on distant continents. A lighthouse was established in 1860 at North Head on Grand Manan Island. There were minor alterations in 1980, but the tower is the original structure. The station was automated in 1986 ; the keeper's house is now a bed and breakfast.

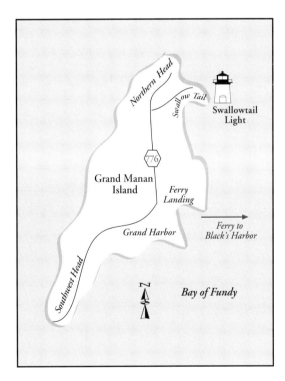

Directions: Ferry to Grand Manan departs from Black's Harbour. The lighthouse is visible on entry to the ferry landing; turn right at landing, then follow Route 776 up hill to the light.

Gannet Rock Light

Built 1831 and one of the most exposed lighthouses in
Canada, Gannet Rock is a mere stone islet, about nine miles
south of Grand Manan Island. The island is named after the
birds that once nested there and is so small that the 91-foot
lighthouse is almost a wave-swept tower. The site for the lighthouse was found to be eight feet lower at one end
than the other and leveling meant blasting into solid rock. The building stone for the base structure was brought to
Gannet Rock by schooner; each stone weighed about
four tons. One of the workers who helped build the
stone-based structure, W. B. McLaughlin, was also a
keeper for 35 years.

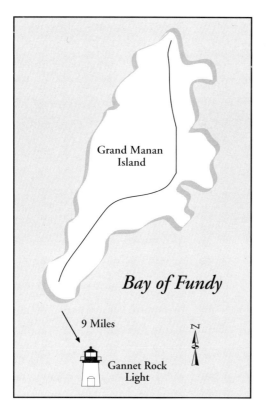

Grand Manan
Island

Bay of Fundy

9 Miles

N
S

Gannet Rock
Light

That the wooden tower has lasted through 168 years of harsh conditions is a testament to its builders; it is the second oldest wooden lighthouse still in use in Canada. The birds, however, disappeared with the construction of the lighthouse. Now in the Grand Manan Museum, the 1906 second-order Fresnel lens was removed in 1967 and replaced with an aerobeacon. The station was destaffed in 1996.

1906 second-order lens

Photos ©Chris Mills

L'Etete Passage Light

Established in 1879, L'Etete Passage light is one of few in New Brunswick with a keeper's house still remaining at the station.

Directions: In St. George, follow signs to Deer Island Ferry. Turn left onto Green's Point Rd. just before ferry landing; continue to the road's end and small parking area.

Pea Point Light

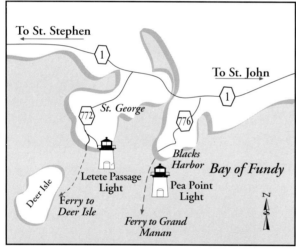

The light at Pea Point was established 1878 and altered in 1965. It is now one of many with a square tower attached at the corner to a small square building. It continues to guide the Grand Manan ferry and local vessels into the harbor.

Directions: From route 1, take the exit to Blacks Harbor and Grand Manan ferry. Follow Route 776; just before reaching the ferry landing there is a turn out area and gate to the left. The lighthouse is about 1/2 mile from the gate--accessible only at low tide.

Drews Head Light

The original light, established 1875, has been replaced with a modern circular, fiberglass structure of utilitarian design.

Directions: Follow Route 776 into Beaver Harbor. Turn at Lighthouse Rd and continue to gate.

Directions: Off Route 1 at Point Lepreau. The lighthouse is on the grounds of the Point Lepreau Generating Station; there is no public access

Point Lepreau Light

Established in 1831, this light is among those lighting the Bay of Fundy Shore. The horizontal red bands are a readily identifiable daymark.

Musquash Head Light

The light was established 1879 and altered in 1959. The single horizontal red band distinguishes it from nearby Point Lepreau Light. The station was destaffed in 1987.

Directions: From Route 1, take the Lorneville exit (Route 100); continue past the plant until a dirt road bears to the right. Follow that road for about 1/2 mile. The path to the lighthouse is marked by a gate on the left; the light is about 1/2 mile from the gate.

Cape Spencer Light

Note map location for Musquash Head Light, previous page; map location for Cape Spencer Light, opposite page

The light at Cape Spencer, established 1872, is now a similar modern structure to that at Drews Head.

Directions: In St. John, follow Union St. through the downtown area, past an industrial area. Turn east onto Red Head Road; continue to a "T" intersection. Turn left and continue to the road's end and parking area.

Partridge Island & Saint John Harbor Lights

The earliest recorded lighthouse on the Bay of Fundy was on Partridge Island at the entrance to Saint John Harbor. Although first lit in 1791, the light subsequently went into disuse and may have been partially dismantled. The original lighthouse was destroyed by fire in 1832. In 1859 the second lighthouse was equipped with North America's first steam-powered fog whistle; a third lighthouse on the island was operational from 1880 until it was replaced with the present concrete tower in 1959.

Saint John was once a traditional gathering site for Maliseet Indians who likely were witness to Samuel de Champlain's arrival in 1604. During the 18th century, the French fortified the city but then lost control to the English. Fort Howe was erected near the homes of two Boston merchants who arrived in the 1760s and established Saint John as the commercial center of the province, with shipbuilding and lumbering industry.

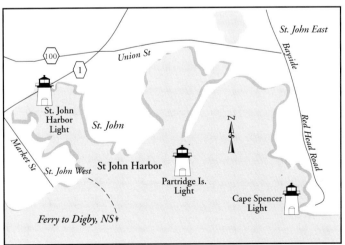

Fort Howe

Continued, following page

Partridge Island & St. John Harbor Lights

Loyalists first landed here May 10,1783 and, in 1784, the first immigration station in Canada was established on the island. Partridge Island became the Canadian equivalent of Ellis Island off New York City. During the 1800s, large numbers of Scottish and Irish immigrants arrived; in the spring and summer of 1847 alone, more than 16,000 passed through the quarantine station. In total, three million immigrants landed between the years 1785-1942. About 50% moved on to the United States and of those who remained in Canada, most moved west rather than remaining in New Brunswick. Some 2000 are buried on the island in six graveyards. A Celtic cross was erected for the Irish refugees and a memorial stone commemorates Jewish immigrants. From the early 1800s to 1947 the island was actively used as a military fortification.

An effort was undertaken to renovate the keeper's house for display of documents and photographs of the island's history, with guided trips offered. However, in recent years landing facilities have been washed out and the property vandalized. Only the foundations of some buildings remain; other decaying structures are succumbing to the elements. There is no public access at present.

The harbor light is on the grounds of the Coast Guard station in Saint John and contains a 4th order Fresnel lens originally in the Brier Island, NS. light.

Directions: From Route 1 take the Market Square exit to the waterfront in downtown St. John. The light is on the grounds of the Coast Guard station.

Quaco Head Light

Marking the headland just east of St. Martins, the lighthouse was established in 1855. It is now representative of the functional design with square tower attached at the corner to a small square structure.

Directions: Follow Route 111 to St. Martins. Turn on West Quaco (Quaco Head) Rd; turn left onto dirt road at Quaco Head Light sign. Continue to the end of the road and parking area.

Cape Enrage Light

Located atop the steep cliffs at Cape Enrage, the light was established in 1840.

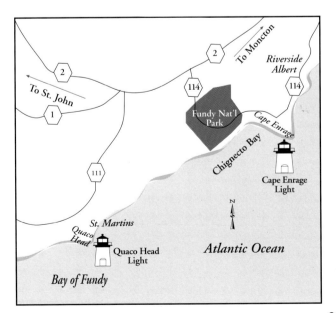

Directions: From Route 2, take the Route 114 exit; continue through Fundy National Park to Route 915. Continue to dirt road to Cape Enrage (turn right) and follow to its end. From Moncton, follow Route 114 to 915; continue to directional sign to the Cape (turn left and follow the road to the light).

Oak Point Light

Established in 1869, the light was altered in 1896. It is located in Oak Point Park and houses a craft shop in season.

Directions: From Route 7, take the Grand Bay or Welsford exit to Route 102; continue to Oak Point. The park entrance is well marked

Bayswater Light

The small pepper shaker light was established 1914 to mark the entrance to Milkish Creek on the Kennebecasis River.

Directions: Take the Grand Bay ferry to Kingston Peninsula. From the ferry landing follow Route 845 to first "T" intersection; turn right and continue to Bayswater. The light is at the road.

Lighthouses of the St. John River Valley

The St. John River from St. John to Fredericton winds through lush farms and hillsides. Unique to this area are the toll free ferries along the river which are part of the New Brunswick highway system. Lighthouses along the river are not always easy to locate and are best seen from the water; only a few are pictured. When paddle steamers travelled the St. John River, the lights were important aids; now many structures have fallen into disuse or have been converted for seasonal use.

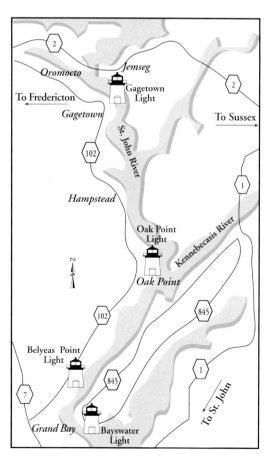

Gagetown Light

Established in 1895 the light is located at the ferry landing, Gagetown.

Directions: Follow Route 102 to Gagetown, turning at the ferry landing

Belyeas Point Light

The light was established in 1882; it is located in Morrisdale on Route 102 off Beach Rd.

30

Northern and Acadian Shores
Cape Tormentine to Chaleur Bay

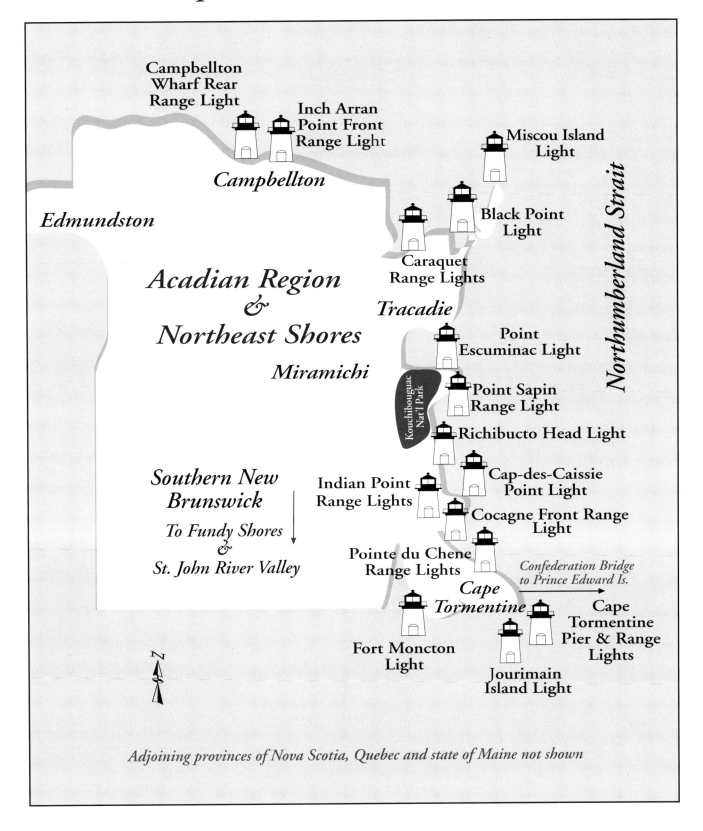

Campbellton
Wharf Rear
Range Light

Inch Arran
Point Front
Range Light

Campbellton

Miscou Island
Light

Edmundston

Black Point
Light

Northumberland Strait

*Acadian Region
&
Northeast Shores*

Caraquet
Range Lights

Tracadie

Miramichi

Point
Escuminac Light

Kouchibouguac Nat'l Park

Point Sapin
Range Light

Richibucto Head Light

*Southern New
Brunswick*

To Fundy Shores
&
St. John River Valley

Indian Point
Range Lights

Cap-des-Caissie
Point Light

Cocagne Front Range
Light

Pointe du Chene
Range Lights

*Confederation Bridge
to Prince Edward Is.*

*Cape
Tormentine*

Cape
Tormentine
Pier & Range
Lights

Fort Moncton
Light

Jourimain
Island Light

N

Adjoining provinces of Nova Scotia, Quebec and state of Maine not shown

Jourimain Island Light

Located on the southeast end of Jourimain Island, the light was established 1870. The white, wooden octagonal tower has unique embellishments around the top deck. The tower has been noted by the Federal Heritage Buildings Review Office as a "Recognized Heritage" structure for these features.

Directions: Turn east onto the first road before the Confederation Bridge on the New Brunswick side, then immediately left onto a dirt road leading into a wildlife area. The lighthouse is about 3/4 mile from the gate; the road and a foot path continue to the light. Views also are possible from the bridge.

Cape Tormentine Pier & Range Lights

Once a busy crossroads for ferry traffic to and from Prince Edward Island, Cape Tormentine is now a quiet village. The range lights were established in 1901. Although the ferry no longer runs, the lights guide local vessels into the harbor.

Range Light

Directions: Follow Route 16, 955 or 960 to the village of Cape Tormentine. The lights are at the old ferry landing.

Pier Light

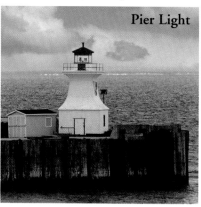

Fort Moncton Light

Established in 1908, the light is a circular, fiberglass tower three meters tall on a raised concrete base. The site is that of an historic earth work fort which dates to the French and English conflicts for control of the New World.

Directions: From the rotary at the intersertion of Rt 16 and 15, follow the signs into Port Elgin. The light is in the park area.

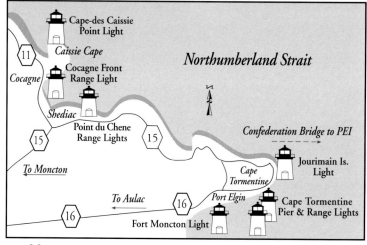

Shediac Range Lights
(Pointe du Chene)

Established in 1895, both towers are traditional wooden structures painted white with the red vertical daymark stripe on front. The front tower is 8.2m; the rear tower is 11.9m. In 1990 the rear tower was relocated back behind the dunes.

Directions: In Parlee Beach Park, Shediac (off Route 15, Exit 37). Follow directional signs to the park.

Cocagne Front Range Light

Established in 1902, the light is a typical small "pepper shaker" style wooden structure.

Directions: On Route 134, on the south side of Cocagne River mouth. The light is near the roadside.

Cap-des-Caissie
Point Light

(Note map locations for these lights on previous page)

The light at Cap-des-Caissie was established in 1872. Originally the dwelling was attached to the wooden tower, but was relocated in 1980. The 11.9m tower is listed as a "Recognized Structure" by the Federal Heritage Buildings Review Office.

Directions: At the end of Caissie Cape, route 530. Turn into "Lighthouse Rd" (visible from main road also).

Richibucto Head Light

Established in 1864 with an attached dwelling, the lighthouse is now a square, tapered wooden tower of "pepper shaker" design. The attached keeper's dwelling was removed in the 1960s.
Directions: On Route 505 near Richibucto Village, on Cap-Lumiere

Dixon Point Light

A light at Dixon Point was established in 1881. The typical, square, tapered tower was built in 1919 and has been moved several times to conform to a shifting channel.
Directions: On Route 535 at Dixon Point, located on private property

Indian Point Range Lights

Directions: On Route 475, north of Bouctouche village.

The present front range light at Indian Point is unusually short and almost triangular in shape. The original light was established in 1883. The rear range light is in the woods, across the road.

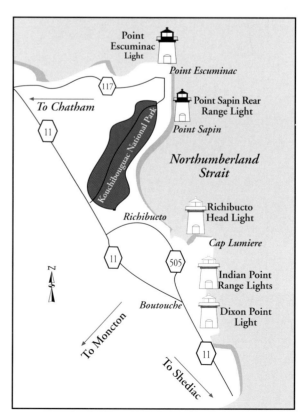

Point Sapin Rear Range Light

Of typical classic design, the structure is a wooden, square, tapered tower. The light was first established in 1941. **Directions:** On Route 117 at Point Sapin.

Point Escuminac Light

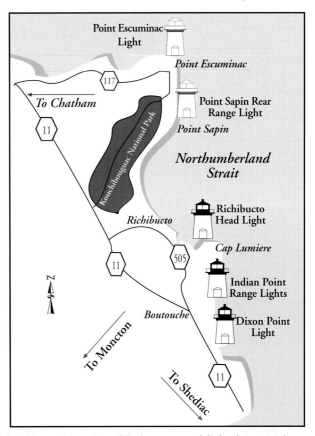

Located at the south side of the entrance to the Miramichi River, the original light was established in 1894 at the end of Escuminac Point. The present modern 20m tower was built in 1971 and automated 1987.
Directions: From Route 117 at Escuminac; turn east and follow road to the end of Escuminac Point. This road can become impassable and four wheel drive is advisable.

Miscou Island Light

At the tip of Miscou Island, the light was established in 1856, and contains the only rotating Fresnel lens in New Brunswick. The area is a park and the lighthouse is open for tours in season. From the tower the Gaspe Peninsula is clearly visible.
Directions: On Miscou Island, on Route 113 at the end of Birch Point. Follow directional signs.

Black Point Light

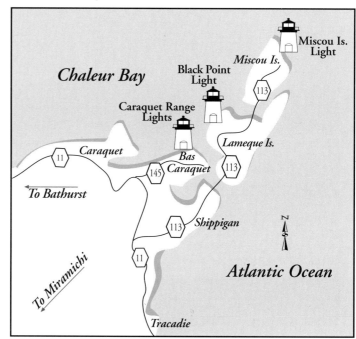

Built in 1967, the steel skeleton tower marks the entrance to Miscou Harbor. It is the most recently built lighthouse in the province.

Directions: Off Route 113 near Petit Shippagan on Isle Lameque. The top of tower is visible from Route 113 and guides you to a secondary road to the light.

Campbellton Wharf Rear Range Light

Established 1879, the original square skeleton tower has been camouflaged. In 1985 the City of Campbellton built a youth hostel around the steel tower, creating the traditional-appearing lighthouse with attached dwelling.

Directions: On Waterfront Drive, adjacent to the Civic Center in Campbellton.

Caraquet Range Lights

Built in 1903, both are square wooden towers with vertical daymark.
Directions: In Bas Caraquet, Route 145. The rear light is just off the road, the front light at the waterfront off a dirt road (visible from main road).

Inch Arran Point Light

Note map location for Caraquet lights, previous page

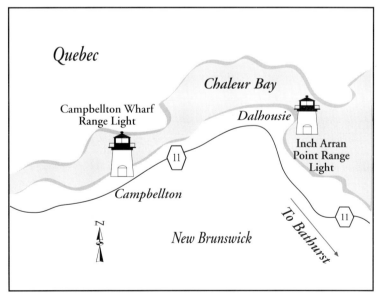

The light was established in 1873 and originally called Bon Ami Point Light. The unique iron railing and stabilizer bars distinguish this light from many of this typical design.

Directions: In Dalhousie at Inch Arran Park

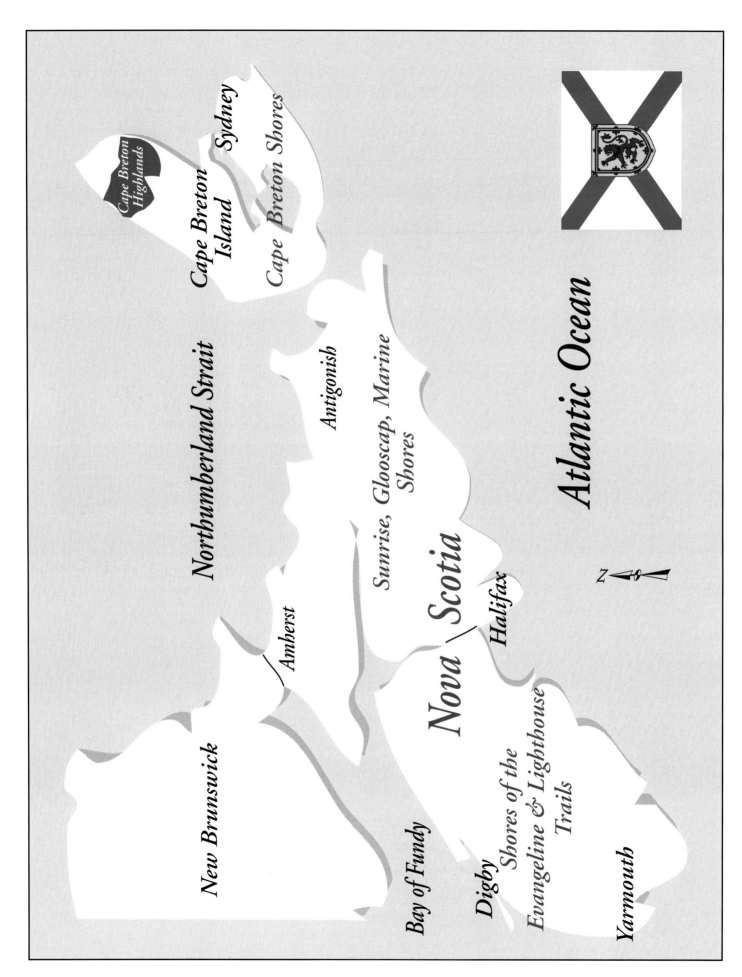

Cape Breton Highlands

Sydney

Cape Breton Island

Cape Breton Shores

Northumberland Strait

Antigonish

Sunrise, Glooscap, Marine Shores

New Brunswick

Amherst

Nova Scotia

Halifax

Atlantic Ocean

N

Bay of Fundy

Digby

Shores of the Evangeline & Lighthouse Trails

Yarmouth

Minas Channel

Bay of Fundy

Atlantic Ocean

Horton Bluff
Front Range Light

Halifax

Peggy's Cove

Peggy's Point
Light

Black Rock
Light

Margaretsville
Point Light

Port George
Light

Hampton
Light

Kentville

Cross Island
Light

Lunenburg

Medway Head
Light

Coffin Island
Light

Annapolis
Royal Light

Schafners
Point
Light

Victoria Beach
Light

Annapolis
Royal

Evangeline Shores
and the
Lighthouse Trail

Fort Point
Light

Liverpool

Western Head
Light

Prim Point
Light

Digby

Bear River
Light

Boars Head
Light

Digby Neck

Gilbertts Cove
Light

Belliveau Cove
Light

Kejimkujik
National
Park

Baccaro Point
Light

Grand Passage
(Northern Point)
Light

St. Mary's Bay

Church Point
Light

Yarmouth

Abbotts
Harbor Light

Seal Island
Light Museum

Barrington

Cape Sable
Light

Brier Island
Light

Cape St. Mary's
Light

Cape Forchu
Light

Bunker Island Light

Clarks
Harbor

Pubnico
Harbor Light

Seal Island
Light

← Ferries to Bar Harbor
and Portland, Maine

N

39

Cape Forchu (Yarmouth) Light

Sailing by the southern tip of Nova Scotia in 1604, Samuel de Champlain called the rocky headland Cape Forchu, "Forked Cape", noting that it pointed threateningly into the sea. Three bodies of water--Yarmouth Harbor, the Gulf of Maine and the Bay of Fundy--surround the Cape. Since 1839 a light has

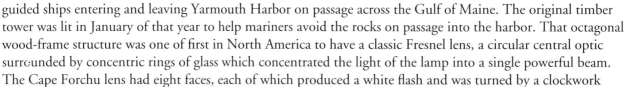

guided ships entering and leaving Yarmouth Harbor on passage across the Gulf of Maine. The original timber tower was lit in January of that year to help mariners avoid the rocks on passage into the harbor. That octagonal wood-frame structure was one of first in North America to have a classic Fresnel lens, a circular central optic surrounded by concentric rings of glass which concentrated the light of the lamp into a single powerful beam. The Cape Forchu lens had eight faces, each of which produced a white flash and was turned by a clockwork mechanism which had to be rewound every three hours. The first lighting apparatus was a kerosene lamp, later replaced by a pressurized vapor lamp, then finally by electricity.

C.1919

Continued, following page

In 1961 the Coast Guard decided the wooden tower must be replaced. Area residents were assured the new tower would be an outward replica of the old. However, considerable controversy arose when the concrete, inverted hexagonal structure began to take form; the new 22.9 meter tower was nicknamed the "apple core". The Fresnel lens was removed during the rebuilding and is now at the Yarmouth County Museum in Yarmouth. Two aerobeaon-style lenses replaced the Fresnel optic in 1962; at two million candlepower, the light was visible 22 miles to seaward. In 1980, Cape Forchu became the monitoring station for approximately 20 automated lighthouses on the South Shore. Following automation in 1993, monitoring was transferred to L'Etete, New Brunswick and Cape Forchu was the last station to be destaffed in Nova Scotia. In 1998 the fog horn was removed and the light downgraded. The Friends of the Yarmouth Light Society now administers the site; the former keeper's house is a tourist bureau and gift shop.

Directions: Seen when approaching Yarmouth by ferry from Maine. From the ferry landing, go north one block to Main St., turn left onto Vancouver St., then left again onto Route 304. Continue to a sign indicating Cape Forchu to the left. Follow that road to the end and the lighthouse. The original Fresnel lens is housed in the Yarmouth County Museum, 22 Collins St.

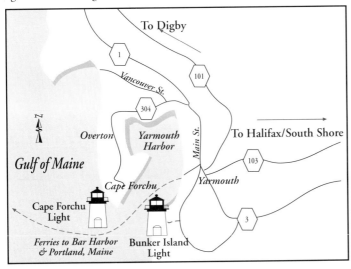

Bunker Island Light

Built on Bunker Island in 1874, the original lighthouse was a wooden structure. A dwelling was also constructed to quarantine sailors who arrived with smallpox. The "pest house" then became the keepers house when a local hospital was completed with facilities for smallpox cases. The present square tower replaced the wooden tower in 1960.

Directions: From Main St. in Yarmouth, continue south approximately 3.6km (2.2mi). Turn right at the sign for Sand Beach (also Bunker Is. sign). Bear left up the hill to a parking area. The light is accessible at low tide.

Abbotts Harbor Light

Located in West Pubnico, the lighthouse is of the traditional "pepper shaker" design. The area's first light was a lantern placed on a mast and located at the south end of Abbotts Island in 1884. The present lighthouse was built to aid local fishermen; it was electrified in 1951 and automated in 1966. The fixed green light is visible for eight nautical miles (15km). The surrounding grounds offer a park and picnic area.

Directions: Follow Route 335 south from West Pubnico about 5km (3mi); turn right onto a paved road marked Abbotts Harbor. Continue about 1.5km (0.9mi) to a small park (sign indicates Lighthouse Park). The light is just past the gate beyond the gravel parking area.

Pubnico Harbor Light

The original lighthouse was built in 1854 on Beach Point, then rebuilt in 1908. Large boulders form a breakwater along the seaward side of the gravel bar which now protects the present red and white circular fiberglass tower. The light is among those scheduled to be decommissioned.

Directions: At the Yarmouth/Shelburne county division on Route 3 in Charlesville, turn onto a gravel road (if driving east, a sign marks Lighthouse Rd). Continue 0.3km (1.8mi) to a gate. The walk to the lighthouse is along the dirt road crossing the gravel bar.

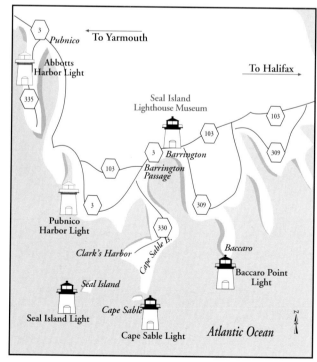

Cape Sable Light

Cape Sable is a low, sandy islet about three miles long, lying just offshore from Cape Sable Island at the extreme southwest corner of Nova Scotia. The Mi'kmaq name for the island was "Kespoogwitik", meaning "where the land ends"; Portuguese cartographers in 1554 called the area Beusablom (sandy bay). French explorer Samuel de Champlain then referred to the area as "Cap de Sable", which became Cape Sable when New England settlers occupied the land in 1761.

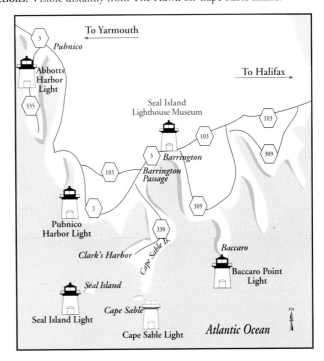

Ledges and shoals run south and west of Cape Sable for 4.5 miles, making all shipping hazardous. Despite loss of vessels and lives, petitions for a lighthouse were ignored until the sinking of the *SS Hungarian* in February, 1860 in which 250 souls perished. The first light tower was built in 1861 close to the southern seawall. Built of wood, the 65 foot octagonal tower was first lit in November of that year, showing a red light. Visibility was only eight miles or less due to the thick red glazing of the lantern.

In 1869 the lantern glazing was changed to clear and red chimneys were installed on the 19 lamps. A clockwork mechanism was installed in 1870 and the light changed to white. A fog alarm building and steam whistle were added in 1876; the lantern received a third-order Fresnel lens in 1902. Because the tower was located on a low land base, it was not visible far enough to seaward. Thus, in 1923/24 a new concrete tower was constructed. At 101 feet, it is the tallest lighthouse in Nova Scotia.

The station was automated in 1986; all buildings except the tower were burned. In 1989 the Federal Heritage Building Review Office designated the Cape Sable Light tower a classified structure, providing it with highest level of ongoing protection.

Directions: Visible distantly from The Hawk on Cape Sable Island.

Photos © Chris Mills

Seal Island Light

Seal Island is the largest of a group of islands located off the southwest tip of Nova Scotia at the "elbow of the Bay of Fundy", where the broad mouth of the bay meets the waters of the open Atlantic. Explorer Samuel de Champlain first recorded the islands in 1604, naming them for the large number of seals there. For more than three hundred years, scores of vessels have succumbed to storms, fog and powerful tides, wrecked on the island and its surrounding ledges. Seal Island is recorded as one of Atlantic Canada's most dangerous shipping areas, with at least 160 vessels lost. The area still commands the respect of all mariners as the freighter *Fermont* ran aground here in 1991.

By the early 19th century, the number of shipwrecks occasioned a grim spring tradition; preachers and residents from Yarmouth and Barrington would come to the island to find and bury the dead. In 1817 Richard Hichens was shipwrecked on Cape Sable, fortunately survived the ordeal and later married Mary Crowell, daughter of a Barrington preacher. Together they settled on the island and established a lifesaving station. In time, the Crowells were joined by Edmund and Joshua Crowell and John Nickerson. The families sheltered and fed shipwreck victims, saving countless mariners from death by exposure.

In 1823 the Nova Scotia House of Assembly voted an annual stipend to support the rescue work. Later the provincial government allocated funds for lifeboats, equipment and additional manpower; the family venture became a fully recognized lifesaving station, the first of only a few built in Canada. The establishment of a lighthouse on Seal Island was due in large part to lobbying by Mary Crowell; island residents thought many of the shipwrecks could be prevented if a lighthouse was constructed on the island.

They petitioned the governor of the province and he agreed to establish a lightstation there. New Brunswick agreed to pay half the cost of construction since the island is halfway between the Atlantic Ocean and the Bay of Fundy.

Lens in Seal Island Museum, Barrington, NS

Seal Island Light Museum

In 1827 a government-funded wharf was completed, making it easier for lifeboats to attend rescues in the area. Construction of a wooden lighthouse at the southern tip of the island began in 1830; it was placed in service in 1831 with a fixed light. Captain Richard Hichens and Edmund Crowell shared the duties of first lightkeeper, then passed the job on to their sons and grandsons, thereby creating a tenure lasting from 1831-1927. A steam fog whistle was installed in 1870 and the fixed light was replaced in 1907-08 with a second-order revolving mechanism giving three flashes every 15 seconds. Over the years the number of shipwrecks and related loss of life steadily declined and by the early 1900s the lifesaving station was deactivated. The light was electrified in 1959 and a rotating aero-beacon installed in 1978, visible for more than 20 miles. The station was automated in 1990. The Fresnel lens is now housed at the Seal Island Light Museum, operated by the Cape Sable Historical Society.

The lighthouse remains an important guide for vessels navigating the Bay of Fundy to the eastern seaboard of the United States and for fisherman working the local waters. The 67-foot wooden tower on the island is the original structure and the oldest in use in the province.

Photos © Chris Mills

Directions: The Nova Scotia Lighthouse Preservation Society offers a trip to the island each season; an overnite stay is included.(902)-424-6442

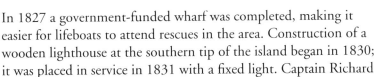

45

Baccaro Point Light

Baccaro Point was named in the 1500s by Basque Fishermen because of the abundant baccalaos (codfish) off its shore. Following petition by local residents, the first lightstation in Barrington Township was first built here in 1850, with the lantern atop a three-storey wooden structure. Placed in service in 1851, the original light was destroyed by fire in 1934 and replaced at that time. In 1955 a keeper's house was constructed. That building was removed when the light was automated in 1984.

Directions: Take the Route 309 exit from Hwy 103 at Clyde River (sign for the lighthouse). Continue about 26km (16mi) through Port Clyde, Upper Port LaTour and Baccaro (always proceed straight). Turn right at Lighthouse Rd; continue 0.6km (.4mi) to the light and parking area.

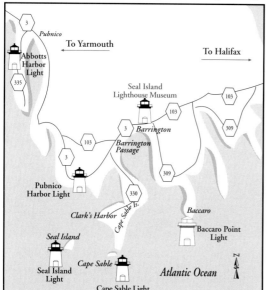

From Barrington on Hwy 103, follow the Lighthouse Route south (sign for Baccaro Light) for 11.5km (7mi). Turn south onto Route 309; continue 6.8km (4.2mi) to Lighthouse Rd. Turn right to the lighthouse.

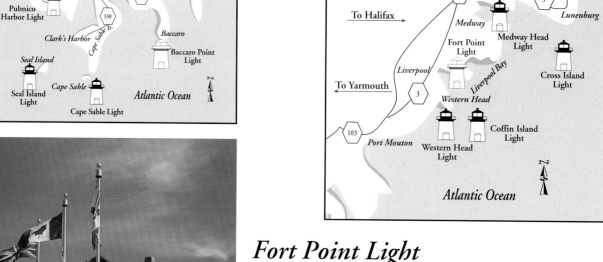

Fort Point Light

A lighthouse was built at this location on the southern shore of Liverpool Bay in 1855 to guide mariners through the harbor into the Mersey River. The first keeper lived in a nearby house rather than at the lighthouse; an attached dwelling later was built, producing an interesting architectural result. In 1928 the original red light was changed to white flashing and the oil lamp replaced with electricity in 1951. The station was automated in 1958 and discontinued in 1989. Now part of the Fort Point Lighthouse Park, the lighthouse is open to visitors in season; displays of lighthouse history and the story of privateers who used Liverpool as home port during the American Revolution and the War of 1812 are featured.

Directions: In Liverpool follow Main St and signs to the park.

Western Head Light

Located at Western Head leading into Liverpool Bay, this light is a relative newcomer. The location was originally established as a fog horn station; the present octagonal concrete tower was built in 1962 and automated in 1988. The site serves as a weather station for Environment Canada.

Directions: From Liverpool on Route 3, turn right onto Bristol Ave, then left onto Main St. and right onto School St. Follow that road for 1.2km (0.7mi) then turn onto Western Head Rd. Continue 7km (4.2mi) to Breakwater St. and turn right; the lighthouse is 0.8km(.5mi) ahead. Roads to Western Head form a loop; you can also continue straight from School St. to Breakwater St., turning left to the light.

Medway Head Light

When built in 1851, the lightstation included a keeper's dwelling with lantern room on top. Iron bars over the windows were an attempt to keep out violent seas. This building is now across the road from the present wooden structure, built in the early 1980s; the original foundation is still visible. The area has been nicknamed Peggy's Cove of Queen's County because of similar rocky, rugged terrain surrounding the lightstation.

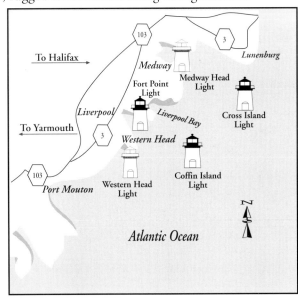

Directions: From Hwy 103, take Exit 17a to Port Medway. Turn south onto Long Cove Rd; continue for approx 5km (3 mi) to the light.

Coffin Island Light

Located on the south point of Coffin Island, this light marks the entrance to the Mersey River and Liverpool Harbor. Built in 1811-12, the original 58-foot wooden tower on a stone foundation was the fifth lighthouse in Nova Scotia. A keeper's dwelling was constructed along with the tower and a year later a lantern and railing were added.

Liverpool was the second most active port in Nova Scotia during the early 1800s, with Coffin Island light the only beacon between Sambro at Halifax and Cape Roseway at Shelburne. The lighthouse stood on the south end of the mile-long island which was only a mile from the nearest mainland village at Beach Meadows. First known as Bear Island, the name was changed in 1817 in honor of Peleg Coffin, a founding settler of Liverpool and large landowner on the island.

James McLeod served as the first keeper, and is credited by some with design of the revolving light mechanism for the Coffin Island lighthouse. The light was powered by whale oil and could be seen for 15 miles.

Photos © Chris Mills

48

Photos © Chris Mills

The first structure stood for more than a century; four red horizontal stripes were added in 1841 and a replacement lantern in 1873. Protective wooden cribwork was placed in 1876 in response to concern about erosion from the sea. In June of 1913, lightning ignited a fire which destroyed the tower and keeper's dwelling. A new 54-foot white octagonal concrete tower was completed in 1914 along with new keeper's quarters. The light was automated in 1962 and the dwelling destroyed in 1964. At that time 100 acres of the island's 130 acres were sold to the province. The federal government now would like to sell the other 30 acres.

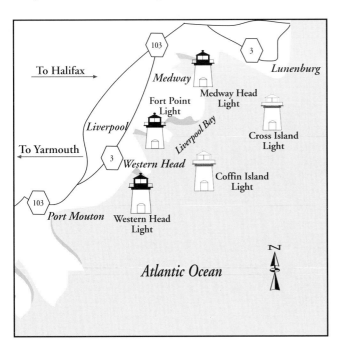

Today the lighthouse is in danger of succumbing to erosion. The Canadian Coast Guard announced plans to replace the light with a buoy and to demolish the present tower, fearing that it would topple into the sea with the next major storm. In an effort to save the historic structure, the newly formed Coffin Island Lighthouse Heritage Society secured a one-year reprieve from the planned demolition. During that time efforts were underway to save the tower and to protect the site. Fund raising was undertaken to subsidize construction of armor rock around the lighthouse to stabilize the site. The rock wall was placed in July, 1999 although only partial funding had been secured; the Society continues its effort to raise the remainder of the required funds.

Directions: The light can be viewed distantly from the beach at Meach Meadows, between Eagle Island and Brooklyn.

Cross Island Light

Former lightkeeper, Chris Mills, notes that Cross Island "sits at the broad mouth of Lunenburg Harbour, some seven miles south of the busy fishing town." He describes the 400-acres as containing "an amazing variety of contrasts: long, sheltered inlets, shale cliffs, quiet woods clearings, rugged shoreline, grassy bluffs and winding trails; a ghost settlement where weathered fish stores and piles of slowly rotting timbers offer the only reminders of a once bustling fishing community."

In the late 1820s merchants, ship owners and fishing interests in Lunenburg petitioned the government for a lighthouse on the island to assist vessels entering the harbor during foul weather. The new light would complete the chain of lights from Sambro to Cape Sable, affording vessels safe passage along the south coast of the province.

Following construction of the lighthouse in 1834, a large black cross was painted on the side of the structure for use as a daymark; the marking also was intended to provide distinction between the beacons at Sambro and Liverpool. In 1835 the lighthouse and keeper's dwelling were painted red to make them yet more identifiable from sea. However, not until 1839 was the beacon lit.

The original tower and other outbuildings burned in 1960; the replacement steel structure was again replaced 20 years later by a modern fiberglass tower. In 1989 the light was automated and is now solarized; the keeper's houses still stand. (**Note map location, previous page**) *Photos © Chris Mills*

Peggy's Point Light

Rising from an outcropping of wave-swept granite and surrounded by large boulders which are among the oldest on the planet, the lighthouse at Peggy's cove is perhaps the most well known of Nova Scotia lighthouses and, to many, symbolizes its maritime spirit. Perched on Peggy's Point, the famous lighthouse draws thousands of visitors, photographers and artists to the rugged, rocky shoreline.

The first lighthouse was built at the entrance to St. Margaret's Bay in 1868. It was a wooden tower atop a keeper's dwelling and displayed a red light. In 1915 the present octagonal concrete tower replaced that original structure. The keeper's house remained for many years, as did a tall flagpole displaying coded black cones and balls to warn of bad weather approaching. Several color and character changes followed, with the most recent being the light color from white to green in 1979. The light was automated in 1958 and the white lantern painted red in 1969.

Surprisingly little is known of the history of this lighthouse, although there are a variety of explanations for the naming of the area. The community may have acquired its name from nearby St. Margaret's Bay, especially since the point marks the eastern entrance; other accounts suggest that "Peggy" was an early settler. A more romantic tale allows that a woman named Peggy was the only survivor of a shipwreck, with many American families claiming descent from the shipwrecked "Peggy".

In summer months a post office is operated at the base of the lighthouse tower, with a lighthouse cancellation stamped on mailings from the site. The community, which becomes thickly congested in summer months, has been declared a preservation site in order to retain the appearance of the fishing village.

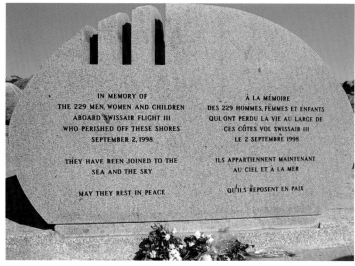

IN MEMORY OF
THE 229 MEN, WOMEN AND CHILDREN
ABOARD SWISSAIR FLIGHT III
WHO PERISHED OFF THESE SHORES
SEPTEMBER 2, 1998

THEY HAVE BEEN JOINED TO THE
SEA AND THE SKY

MAY THEY REST IN PEACE

À LA MÉMOIRE
DES 229 HOMMES, FEMMES ET ENFANTS
QUI ONT PERDU LA VIE AU LARGE DE
CES CÔTES VOL SWISSAIR III
LE 2 SEPTEMBRE 1998

ILS APPARTIENNENT MAINTENANT
AU CIEL ET À LA MER

QU'ILS REPOSENT EN PAIX

Peggy's Point Light (con't)

On September 2, 1998, Swissair flight 111 crashed into the sea 12 miles off Peggy's Cove; first rescuers at the crash site were fishermen from the village. The entire community and neighboring villages participated in the rescue efforts although little mention is now made of those days. A service for the victims was held near the lighthouse and two memorials have now been placed to commemorate the tragic loss of life.

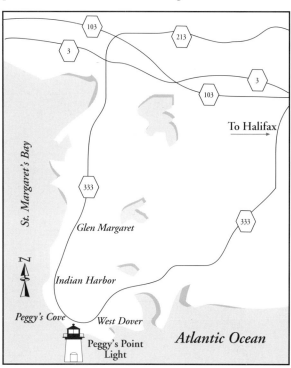

Directions: Follow Hwy 103 from Halifax to Exit 5, then to Route 333 26km(16mi) to Peggy's Cove. Or take Route 333 directly from Halifax. Large parking areas ajoin a restaurant/gift shop; the village is a thickly congested area.

Horton Bluff Front Range Light

On the west side of the Avon River, the light was built in 1851 to guide vessels into Avonport, once known for brick production. An attached keeper's dwelling was added later. The present structure is a typical square tower with attached flat-roof building. A vertical fluorescent red stripe is the range light marking. The rear range light is a skeleton tower.

Directions: Take Exit 9 off Highway 101 (Avonport). Turn left, then right. Continue to Bluff Road and turn right; proceed about 2 miles (3.2km) to Lighthouse Rd and turn left. The light is immediately ahead across the railroad tracks.

Black Rock Light

On the south shore of Minas Channel, a modern circular tower with horizontal red daymark stripes replaced the original 1848 lighthouse. The original foundation was used for the present structure.

Directions: Take Exit 15 from Highway 101; continue north on Route 360. At the intersection in Welsford, turn onto 221 East. Follow that road 3.5mi (5.4km) to Grafton, turn north and continue about 6 miles (10km). Turn right onto a gravel road and continue to the lighthouse.

Margaretsville Point Light

Located on a small headland which projects into the Bay of Fundy, the square, white wooden structure with black horizontal band, was established in 1859, one of the first on the Nova Scotia side of the Bay of Fundy. At nearby Peter's Point, wrecker Peter Barnes fell to his death 20 years after luring a schooner to a tragic end at that spot.

Directions: From Highway 101, take Exit 18A. Turn north onto Route 362 and continue about 1mi (1.5km); turn right, then left to continue on 362 into the village. The light is just past the Community Hall to the left.

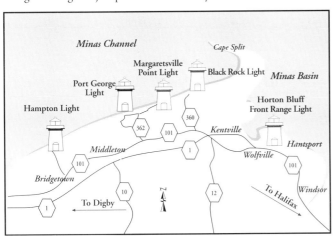

Port George Light

Annapolis Royal Light

The Port George light was built in 1888 and sits between the road and the low shoreline. It is of standard "pepper shaker" design.

Directions: At Exit 18 from Highway 101, turn onto Rt 362. Continue to signs directing you to Port George. The secondary road makes a loop down toward the water and the hamlet of Port George; the lighthouse is at the road.

Built in 1889, the Annapolis Royal light still functions, with the lantern showing fixed red to guide mariners on the Annapolis River. During the season the structure operates as a tourist information center

Directions: From Highway 101, follow the Annapolis Royal exit to Route 8 (St. George St.). From Rt. 1, turn north onto St. George St. Continue into the center of town; the lighthouse is just past Fort Anne.

Map location, following page

Hampton Light

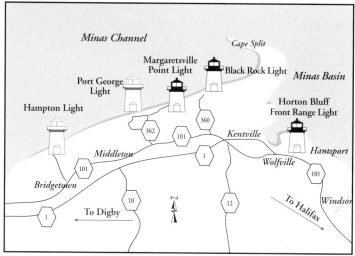

Constructed in 1911 of similar design to others on the Bay of Fundy, this light guides mariners into Chute Cove.

Directions: Take Exit 20 from Highway 101, continue on Rt. 1 into Bridgetown on Church St. Follow Church St/Hampton Mt. Rd. for 6 miles; turn left and continue about 0.5mi. (0.8km). Turn right onto the road to Hampton Beach and follow it to the light.

Schafners Point Light

This lighthouse was constructed in 1885 to warn mariners of the dangerous shoals surrounding nearby Goat Island. The tapered wooden tower is now adjacent to the roadside; the red octagonal lantern shows a fixed white beam. Immediately to the east of Schafners Point is the Habitation at Port Royal, a reconstruction of the original site built in 1605. Now a National Historic Site, the Habitation was the earliest European settlement north of Florida.

Directions: At Annapolis Royal, turn east onto Route 1. A sign directs you back westward toward Port Royal; follow this road to Schafners Point and the light.

Victoria Beach Light

Established in 1901, the small pepper-shaker style tower is located on a steep hillside on the east side of Digby Gut. The ferry from Digby to St. John, NB passes the light.

Directions: Turn off Route 1 just east of Annapolis Royal onto the road leading to Port Royal (marked). Continue past Schafners Point to the road's end, keeping right at the "Y", then bearing left down a steep hill. The light is located behind a private home.

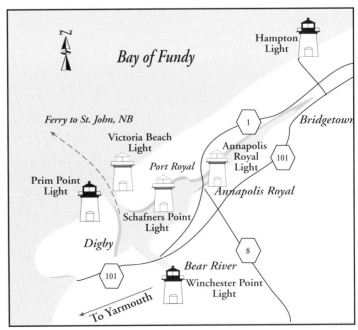

Prim Point Light

Point Prim is a rocky headland and the west entrance point for Digby Gut, the deep water passage which leads to the Annapolis Basin. The original 1817 lightstation was a square, tapering tower atop a 1-1/2 storey keeper's house. When rebuilt in the 1870s, a red daymark stripe was painted on the tower and house. The present square, white tower retains the vertical red stripes. In 1987 the station was destaffed.

Directions: In Digby, follow Route 303 north toward the ferry landing. Continue past the intersection with Route 217; turn left at the intersection with Lighthouse Rd, then immediately right. Follow that road 7.4km (4.6 mi) to the lighthouse.

Winchester Point Light

Of typical pepper shaker style, the light was built in 1906 when the town of Bear River was an important lumbering and shipbuilding center. The 20 feet tides allowed large schooners to navigate the river into the village wharfs.

Directions: From Route 101, take Exit 24. At the stop sign turn right; the first or second narrow dirt road will take you to the light.

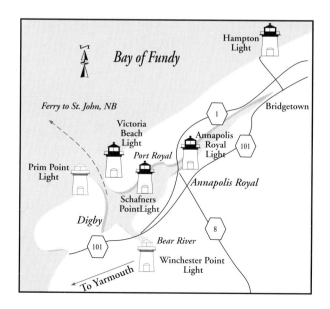

Boars Head Light

A lighthouse was established here in 1864 to aid fishing and commercial vessels which once dominated traffic in the Bay of Fundy. Tiverton is now a small fishing port on Long Island.

Directions: Follow Route 217 to East Ferry, take the ferry to Long Island. At Tiverton turn right, following the paved road up the hill. Continue past the gate (walk or drive) 0.6 mi (1km) to the light.

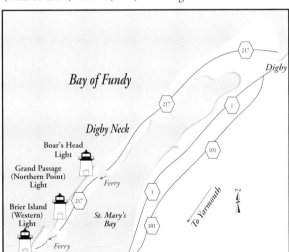

Grand Passage Light

Located at the northern point of Brier Island, this light was established in 1901 to aid navigation into Grand Passage from the Fundy side of Digby Neck. Although destaffed in 1988, a Coast Guard lifeboat is now based there and keeper's quarters used by staff.

Directions: From the ferry dock at Westport, Brier Is., turn right onto Water St. Continue to the road's end at the light

Brier Island Light

Also known as Western Light, the tower was built 1809 at the tip of a narrow peninsula known as Digby Neck, enclosing St. Mary's Bay. Entrance to the harbor is so narrow that even local mariners have difficulty. The original tower was rebuilt in 1832, and the present lighthouse built in 1944 after the previous structure burned. The light was destaffed in 1987.

Directions: At Digby follow Rt. 217 along Digby Neck to Brier Island (taking two small ferries en route). Turn left from the ferry, continue 0.4mi (.6km) then bear right onto Wellington St. At the pavement's end turn left onto the gravel road; continue 2.2mi (3.7km) to the lighthouse.

Gilberts Cove Light

Gilberts Cove was part of an active lumber shipping district, supplying materials for shipbuilding and export. A lightkeeper's house with lantern room on top was built on Gilberts Point in 1904. Decline in the shipping and fishing industries prompted closure of the keeper's dwelling and automation of the light in the late 1960s.

In 1982 the Gilberts Cove and District Historical Society was formed and the community obtained custody of the lighthouse. It is now a Nova Scotia Heritage Property; the interior has been renovated and includes a gift shop.

Directions: On Gilberts Point. Turn off Route 101 onto Lighthouse Rd. and continue to the parking area.

Cape St. Marys Light

The original lighthouse at Cape St. Marys was built in 1868 on the east side of the bay. Today the structure is one of the many square concrete towers attached to the corner of a small square building. Remains of the keeper's house can be seen in the field near the station.

Directions: Follow Route 1 into Mavillette, turning onto the Cape St. Mary Rd. Continue approximately 1.8 miles (3km), turn right onto a gravel road; the lighthouse is just ahead.

Belliveau Cove Light

The small pepper shaker light is located at the end of the town wharf, marking the harbor entrance. **Directions:** Just off Route1 in the village.

Church Point Light

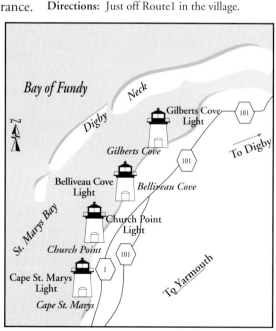

The small lighthouse overlooking St. Mary's Bay was built in 1874. No longer active, the Universite Sainte-Anne maintains the light and grounds.

Directions: In the village of Church Point, turn off Route 1 onto Lighthouse Rd. which passes university buildings. Continue past the gate onto a gravel road which ends at the lighthouse.

58

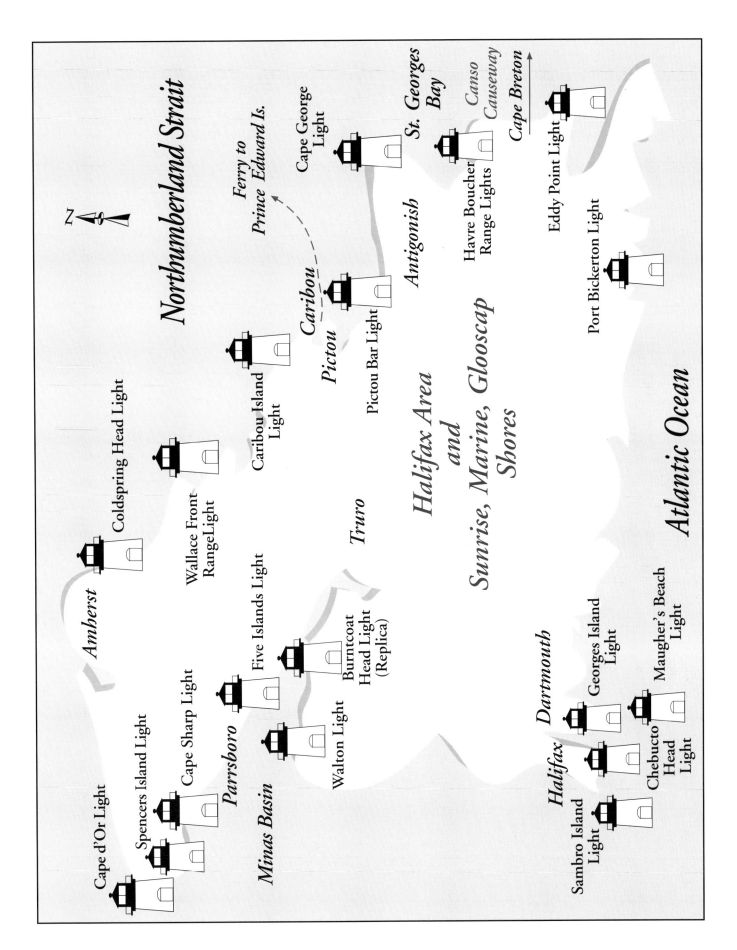

Northumberland Strait

N

Ferry to
Prince Edward Is.

Cape George
Light

St. Georges
Bay

Canso
Causeway

Cape Breton

Caribou

Pictou

Antigonish

Havre Boucher
Range Lights

Eddy Point Light

Coldspring Head Light

Caribou Island
Light

Amberst

Wallace Front
RangeLight

Pictou Bar Light

Halifax Area
and
Sunrise, Marine, Glooscap
Shores

Port Bickerton Light

Cape Sharp Light

Parrsboro

Five Islands Light

Truro

Atlantic Ocean

Spencers Island Light

Minas Basin

Burntcoat
Head Light
(Replica)

Dartmouth

Georges Island
Light

Maugher's Beach
Light

Cape d'Or Light

Walton Light

Halifax

Chebucto
Head
Light

Sambro Island
Light

59

Sambro Island Light

Sambro Island lighthouse stands on a granite island about two nautical miles outside the entrance to Halifax Harbor, marking an area of dangerous shoals. The second largest ice-free port in the world (only Sydney, Australia is larger), Halifax was founded in 1749 as the major base for the British Navy in North America. Although offering safe haven for a large fleet, the harbor entrance was often masked by fog and more than 30 shoals surrounding Sambro Island represented a grave hazard.

The oldest continuously operational lighthouse in North America, the 1758 tower predates Captain James Cook's around-the-world voyage of exploration (1776-1779) and the American Revolution (1775-1783). Although the French established Canada's first true lighthouse at Louisbourg in 1734, it was destroyed by British cannon when the fortress was taken; nearly a century would pass before that light was rebuilt.

As early as 1752 efforts were made to raise funds for construction of a light on "Cape Sambrough" but without success. In October, 1758, the General Assembly of Nova Scotia passed an act to establish a lighthouse on "Sambro Outer Island". Funds for construction were raised via a tax on "spirituous liquors", a plentiful and popular commodity. A tax on vessels entering the harbor also was instituted. Built of granite with walls 60 feet high and more than five feet thick at the base, the stone tower was intended to withstand wartime. The light was put in service in 1760 and displayed a fixed white light, 115 feet above sea level.

Photos © Chris Mills

Exterior photos preceding and during restoration

Within a few years, reports of inefficiency in operation of Sambro Light reached the Legislative Assembly. Investigation revealed that the keeper had been pocketing duties paid by ships, procuring only the cheapest materials and leaving the light out if no ships were in immediate sight. A recommendation that the government assume operation of Sambro Light did not go forward however.

In 1864 a new iron lantern with plate glass windows and a light with reflectors was installed. At that time serious consideration was given to lowering the tower. A fog signal station was established in the late 18th century. In 1906 a 22-foot octagonal concrete addition to the tower was built, making the tower 74 feet tall. At that time the light was changed from fixed white to flashing. A first-order Fresnel lens also was installed, making Sambro light one of Canada's major coastal beacons.

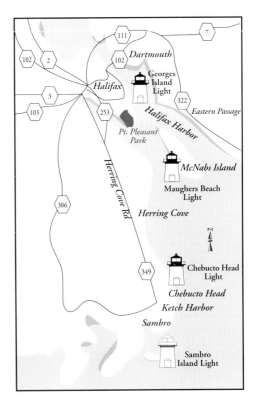

The old stone walls were covered with shingles to protect the mortar from deterioration in the salt air. Originally white, the tower was painted with red stripes to make it more visible in snowy weather. In 1968 the Fresnel lens was replaced with an aerobeacon with a range of 24 miles, flashing every five seconds. The Maritime Museum of the Atlantic in Halifax now displays the 1906 Fresnel lens.

Sambro Island Light

Sambro light was automated in 1988. In 1997 it was designated a protected heritage building and in August, 1998 work commenced to restore the exterior of the lighthouse. The 1906 railings were cut apart, taken down, refurbished and repainted bright red. Other major work included reconstruction/renovation of the tower's wood entryway, entry steps and steps at the top of the tower. New shingles were installed and repainted, restoring the distinctive day mark stripes.

The abandoned 1960s keeper's dwellings still stand but have fallen victim to vandals and were boarded up. All work on the tower was completed in December, 1998 just as the lighthouse marked its 240th year.

Directions: The Nova Scotia Lighthouse Preservation Society offers periodic trips to the island during the season. (902) 424-6442. *Note map location, previous page.*

The lighthouse following 1998 restoration work

Photos © Chris Mills

The lighthouse following 1998 restoration work

Photos © Chris Mills

Chebucto Head Light

A light at Chebucto Head was first built in 1872 to guide vessels into Halifax Harbor. The present 45-foot (14m) concrete structure was built in 1967 and is located 1/2 mile north of Chebucto Head. The original site became a gun and search light battery during World War II.

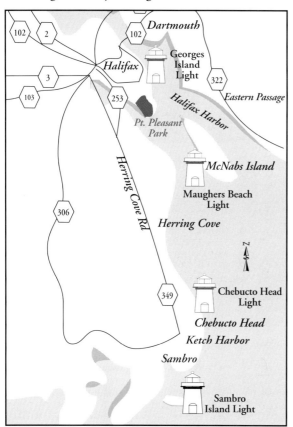

Directions: In Halifax at the Armdale Rotary, follow Route 253 to Herring Cove. Turn onto Route 349, continue 5.5mi (9km) to Duncans Cove (paved road) then bear left. Follow that road 1.5mi (2.2km) to the lighthouse.

64

Maugher's Beach Light

The view seaward from Halifax is marked by the long arm of Maugher's Beach reaching out from McNab's Island, punctuated by a lighthouse. All ships entering the harbor pass within close range and one observer referred to the light as "our own Statue of Liberty". The beach was named for local Halifax merchant and rum distiller, Joshua Maugher, who used the area to dry fish. During the Napoleonic wars the Royal Navy used the beach to hang bodies of executed mutineers as warning to ships entering the harbor.

The British army in 1814 began construction of a stout, round granite tower to house a small cannon battery to defend the harbor entrance. Although the tower was 14 years in the making, a light was shone as early as 1815 when naval ships were expected. A permanent light was voted by the provincial legislature in 1826 and a lantern room was placed atop the existing tower.

Other buildings gradually were added at the end of Maugher's Beach, including a fog alarm (1906), duplex keeper's house (1913) and a variety of outbuildings. Facing the open Atlantic, the beach took the brunt of storms, acting as a breakwater for Halifax Harbor. In 1931 the original granite tower succumbed to a brutal winter storm which ripped much of the outer wall from the south side of the tower. When the tower was rebuilt, wooden pilings and breakwaters were added to contain the erosion of the beach; additional granite boulders were added in 1957 and major reconstruction of the breakwater undertaken in 1987. The present concrete tower was built in 1941; the fog alarm building was demolished in 1975 and the fog alarm relocated to the lighthouse where it remained until discontinued in 1993. Automation of the Maugher's Beach light was planned for 1973 but was not accomplished until 1983. The keeper's house was demolished in 1987; foundations of that structure and the fog alarm building remain.

McNab's Island had another light, built in 1903 on a hill on the northwest corner of the island. At 132 feet, this light had a longer range (17mi) than the Maugher's Beach beacon. Known as the McNab's Island Lighthouse, the tower was incorporated into the center of the keeper's house. This light was automated in 1959 and torn down in 1976; a pair of small red lights on skeleton towers now direct ships on approach into Halifax.

Directions: A seasonal ferry offers trips to McNabs Island leaving from Eastern Passage. There is a clear path to the light and to other points of interest on the island. (*Note map location, previous page*)

Georges Island Light

Photos © Chris Mills

When Halifax was founded in 1749 by Colonel Edward Cornwallis, the island was called George Island, after King George II. In 1963 the name was changed to Georges Island. The first lighthouse was established in 1876, located on the western shore; two fixed white lights were displayed 20 feet apart vertically. The tower was a 35-foot white, square wooden structure with a black diamond daymark on the south side and red iron lantern.

In 1899 the fog bell from the Maugher's Beach Light was transferred to Georges Island and in 1903 the light was changed to one flashing red light at 50 feet high. When the lighthouse was destroyed by fire in 1916, a temporary red occulting light was established and a new concrete lighthouse built in 1917. That tower stands today; nearby is the former lightkeeper's house.

A fourth-order Fresnel lens was installed in 1922. In 1973 a red florescent stripe was painted on the south side of the tower. Today the light is listed as the front light of "Halifax Harbor Inner Range" and shows a fixed white light; the rear range light is on a skeleton tower in Dartmouth, exhibiting an occulting white light. Parks Canada is working on restorations to the island with future plans to open it to the public.

Directions: The light is visible from the Halifax waterfront or on entering Halifax Harbor. (*Note map location, previous page*)

Port Bickerton Light
The Nova Scotia Lighthouse Interpretive Centre

Built in 1901, the original square, two storey keeper's house with lantern room on top still stands at Barachois Head beside the present, operating light. The community of Port Bickerton has renovated the dwelling and square, rooftop lantern; painting, restoration of the hardwood floors and addition of memorabilia reflect the decor of the era. The centre presents the history of Nova Scotia lighthouses and maritime tradition; a short climb to the lantern room affords a spectacular view.

The functioning light is of the strictly utilitarian design: a square concrete tower with red lantern attached to a small building which once housed the foghorn machinery.

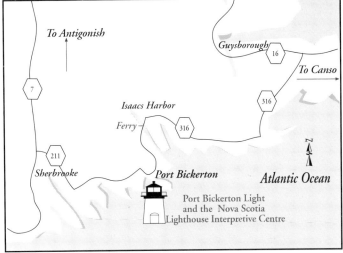

Directions: From Route 211 ("Marine Drive"), follow the directional sign for Lighthouse Rd 3.5km (2mi) to the lighthouse. There is a parking area just below the lighthouse and center.

Port Bickerton is 7km (4.2mi) from the Country Harbor Cable Ferry off Route 316 and about 30 minutes from Sherbrooke Village.

Eddy Point Light

The lighthouse marks the division between Chedabucto Bay and the Strait of Canso, which separates Cape Breton Island from the mainland. The original tower was built in 1851; the remains of the foundation are still visible near the present 8.6m (28ft) fiberglass circular structure.

Directions: Follow Route 344 south to Sand Point. Turn onto a gravel road marked Eddy Point Light and continue to the lighthouse.

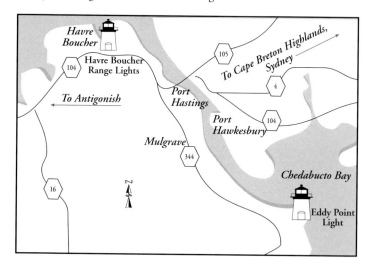

Havre Boucher Front Range Light

Named after Capt. Francis Boucher who spent the winter of 1759 in the area. Havre Boucher is an active fishing community on the Northumberland Strait. The rear range light was constructed in 1842 and front range light in 1879. Both are square wooden towers with vertical red daymark, the front light at the shoreline and rear light on a hill next to private homes.

Directions: Take the Havre Boucher exit from the Trans Canada Highway (104). Following the road into the village; the light is visible across the railroad tracks at the shore and the rear light up the hill.

Cape George Light

St. George's Bay is the largest in Nova Scotia. This region has been referred to as the "mini Cabot Trail", with both Cape Breton and Prince Edward Island visible from the lighthouse in clear weather. The first lighthouse on the point was a lantern atop a wooden dwelling. In 1907 a tower and attached keeper's house were built. The present octagonal concrete tower was built in 1968; the light is shown from 405 feet above sea level.

Directions: From Antigonish (reached via Trans Canada Hwy 104), follow Route 337 north 37km (22.5mi). A dirt road bearing to the right is marked Lighthouse Rd; continue to the road's end and the light.

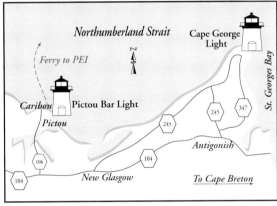

Pictou Bar Light

Built in 1834 to guide sailing ships entering Pictou Harbor, the light is located on a finger of land that projects into the center of the harbor entrance. The vertical red stripes on the harbor side are a typical daymark; the Northumberland Strait is to the north and east.

Directions: On Route 348 from the north, pass Pictou Landing and continue into a small community. Take the first left (directly across from Rose Ave). A small dirt road to the left leads to the beach area. The walk along the sand bar to the light takes about 15 minutes.

Wallace Front Range Light

The original range lights were built in 1904; today the front light remains active as a sector light. Approaching vessels see a narrow white beam when in the proper channel. If diverted too far to the left or right, the light shows green or red respectively, directing the boat back to course. The rear range light was taken out of service years ago and is now part of a private residence.

Directions: The light is located on an embankment directly on Route 6 just east of Wallace.

Caribou Island Light

A lighthouse was established on the northeast end of Caribou Island at Gull Point in 1868. The "island" is actually a long piece of land jutting into the Northumberland Strait. The square tower attached to a small square structure is a common design.

Directions: Follow Route 6 to Caribou River, turning onto the Shore Road (paved);turn north onto Caribou Island Road (gravel) and continue to the light. There are also other turns, marked with signs onRoute 6, which take you to the island road.

Coldspring Head Light

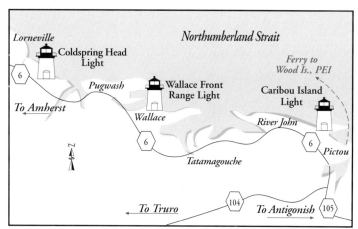

First placed on this sandstone point along the Northumberland Strait in 1890, the lighthouse at Coldspring Head is located in a field, with trees cut out on the water side to guide local fishing boats.

Directions: From Route 366 turn north at Lane #26 (marked), between Northport and Lorneville. A sign indicates Cold Spring Head, Private Road. Continue to a junction, turn right then immediately left. The lighthouse is shortly to the left in a field.

Cape d'Or Light

Cape d'Or ("Cape of Gold") marks the junction of the Bay of Fundy and the Minas Channel. In 1697 Samuel de Champlain named a point just west of this location Cape of Two Bays because the headland divided the Minas Basin from Chignecto Bay. Originally established as a fog horn station in 1875, a lighthouse was established here in 1922 with the current building dating from the 1960s. The design is the typical functional square tower attached to the corner of a small square building. Now a Guest House and restaurant, the two keepers' houses still stand.

Directions: Take Route 209 to East Advocate, turn south onto a paved road directing you to the lighthouse. Turn left onto a gravel road and continue to the lighthouse.

Spencers Island Light

Located on the Minas Channel, this light was instrumental in guiding vessels when the village was an important ship building area. The lighthouse was built in 1904, with a fixed red light visible for seven miles. Sailing vessels would wait in the area for favorable winds to go up or down the Bay of Fundy. There was also heavy barge traffic in the area. The light was discontinued in the 1980s when commercial shipping no longer used the channel. The Spencers Island Community Association later acquired the structure. Major renovations were made in 1995 and 1996; the light has now been designated a municipal heritage structure.

Directions: From Route 209 turn south at the sign for Spencer's Beach. Follow signs to the lighthouse.

Five Islands Light

A small, wooden structure was built at Sand Point in 1912-13 and was established as an unwatched tower in 1914. The original lamp was kerosene fueled. In 1967 the light was electrified and changed to red. Erosion required the lighthouse to be moved back from the shore in 1952 and again in 1957. In 1993 the light was decommissioned and, in 1996, moved to its present location at the Sand Point Campground. The Five Islands Lighthouse Preservation Society maintains the structure.

Directions: At Five Islands on Route 2, turn into the Sandy Point Campground and follow signs to the lighthouse--or continue to the beach area and walk around and up the bluff to the light.

71

Cape Sharp Light

The wooden tapered square tower, built in 1886, originally had keeper's house adjacent. Only a small fog horn building is now located there. The flashing white light has a range of 11 nautical miles and warns mariners of the Cape Blomidon headland nearby. (*Map location, previous page*)

Directions: From the 3-way intersection at the Town Hall in Parrsboro, bear south. Continue for 2mi (3km) to a "Y" intersection and bear right. Follow that road (becomes gravel) approximately 4.5mi (7km). Turn left onto a gravel road leading to cottages; a narrow road at the power line leads to a trail up and over the mountain to the lighthouse.

Burntcoat Head Light (Replica)

On the south side of the entrance to Cobequid Bay, Burntcoat Head was named after an incident in which a local farmer's coat caught fire when he left a pipe in his pocket. The first lighthouse on the head was built in 1858 and lit in 1859, a square wooden tower attached to a wooden keeper's dwelling. Kerosene lamps showed a fixed, white light visible for 13 nautical miles. By 1913 the narrow strip of land connecting Burntcoat Head to the mainland had eroded; the original lighthouse was demolished and a new one built on the mainland. The replacement structure was a white, square wooden dwelling with red lantern atop the roof. A fourth-order Fresnel lens was installed; the light was visible for 14 nautical miles. In 1950 the light was electrified; the building was demolished in 1972 and replaced by a skeleton tower. That light was subsequently discontinued so today there is no navigation marker for the head. The replica, built in 1994 with tourism funding and local fund raising efforts, now offers history of the lighthouse and area.

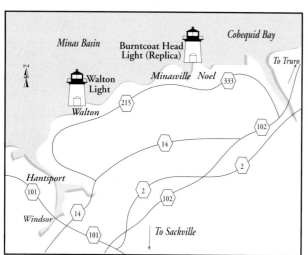

Directions: From Route 215 turn at Noel or Minasville at the Burntcoat Head sign. This road makes a loop to the Burncoat Head Park area.

Walton Light

Once the brightest lighthouse on the upper Bay of Fundy, the present light was built in 1873 to guide seagoing ships into the port of Walton. The wooden structure is of typical tapered design; originally a Fresnel lens magnified the light apparatus consisting of two large, flat wick lamps powered by kerosene. In the 1970s shipping from the port declined and the lighthouse was decommissioned, declared surplus and offered for sale. The Municipality of East Hants purchased the property in 1991 and the lighthouse was given heritage status in 1992. Today the East Hants Tourism Association maintains the structure and grounds.

Directions: Follow Route 215 to the village of Walton. There are signs posted directing to the lighthouse and park area

Cape Breton Shores

Northumberland Strait

Enragee Point Light

Cape Breton Highlands National Park

Neils Harbor Light

Cheticamp

Margaree Harbor Range Lights

Mabou Harbor Light

Cape Breton Island

Henry Island Light

Point Aconi Light

Ferry to Newfoundland

Black Rock Point Light

Sydney Front Range Light

Lake Ainslie

Port Hood

Baddeck

St. Georges Bay

Kidston Island Light

Man of War Point Light

Low Point Light

Sydney

Canso Causeway

Bras d'Or Lake

Louisbourg

St. Peters

Jerome Point Light

Fortress of Louisbourg National Historic Site

Port Hawksbury

Grandique Point Light

Fourchu

Louisbourg Light

Marache Point Light

Fourchu Head Light

N

Atlantic Ocean

Henry Island Light

Located at the entrance to Port Hood, Henry Island Lighthouse was placed in operation in December, 1902 and serves the large number of ships and fishing vessels in the Canso Strait. The wooden tower was built in 1901 along with a keeper's house and outbuildings. Situated at the highest part of the island, the octagonal structure is 195 feet above seal level, 38 feet from the base to vane. In 1902 an oil house was added.

The light, which at one time was visible for 28 nautical miles, now has a six nautical mile range. A radiophone was installed in 1950 and the light automated in 1962. All buildings, save the lighthouse itself, were sold to private ownership. The keeper's dwelling has now been carefully restored and renovated for private use.

Directions: Henry Island is located four miles off Port Hood. The Nova Scotia Lighthouse Preservation Society offers periodic outings to the island. (902)-424-6442

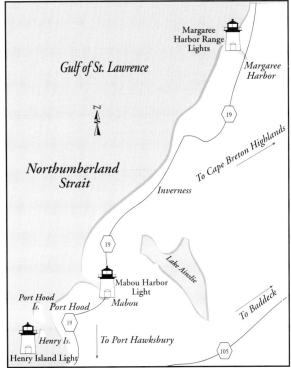

Margaree
Harbor Range
Lights

Gulf of St. Lawrence

*Margaree
Harbor*

19

**Northumberland
Strait**

To Cape Breton Highlands

Inverness

Lake Ainslie

19

*Mabou Harbor
Light*

Mabou

*Port Hood
Is.   Port Hood*

To Baddeck

19

Henry Is.

To Port Hawksbury

105

Henry Island Light

Mabou Harbor Light

In 1884 the government built the 37-foot wooden pyramidal tower as a rear range light to aid fishing vessels entering the wharf. The present light shows fixed yellow.

Directions: From the village of Mabou on Route 19 follow the road marked Mabou Harbor. Continue to the Mabou Harbor Wharf sign (7km/4.2mi); turn left onto the dirt road which ends at the lighthouse and wharf area. (***Map location previous page***)

Enragee Point Light

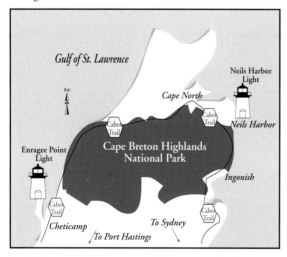

Built in 1937 at the northern tip of Cheticamp Island, Enragee Point light guides mariners in the Northumberland Strait and directs returning fishing vessels into Cheticamp Harbor.

Directions: In Cheticamp, follow the sign indicating "Cheticamp Island". Continue to Island Light Rd., turn right and follow the dirt road that parallels the harbor. Continue to the road's end and the light.

Margaree Harbor Range Lights

Both front and rear range lights were built in 1900 to guide fishing vessels into the harbor and river mouth. Each is a square wooden tower with red lantern and red vertical daymark.

Directions: From Rt 219 follow the signs for Margaree Harbor and the Shore Rd to the end. The lights are visible as you enter the village. (***Map location previous page***)

Neils Harbor Light

The typical pepper shaker style lighthouse was originally built in 1899 to mark the harbor entrance. It is now part of a picnic area.

Directions: From the Cabot Trail, follow the sign to Neils Harbor. Turn onto Lighthouse Road (gravel) and continue to the light. *(Map location previous page)*

Man of War Point Light

This small, pepper shaker style light was built in 1912 on the southwestern shore of Great Bras d'Or Lake, one of the channels connecting Bras d'Or lake to the Atlantic Ocean.

Directions: From the Trans Canada Highway 105, take Exit 13. Continue for approximately 5 miles (8km); turn right onto a narrow dirt road indicated by "Man of War Art Gallery" sign. At the gallery, bear right at the Lighthouse Trail sign. The light is down a trail to the shore.

Black Rock Point Light

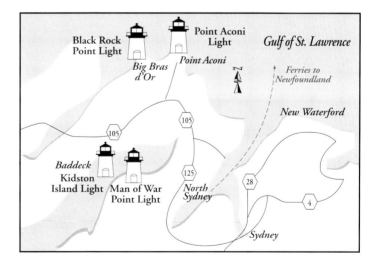

Shipping traffic entering Bras d'Or Lake is guided by Black Rock Point Light. The original light tower and dwelling were built in 1868 with the present structure a functional white square tower attached to foghorn building.

Directions: Take Exit 14 or 15 from Trans Canada 105, continue into Big Bras d'Or. At the Fire Hall turn onto Black Rock Rd; at the end of the pavement turn left onto a dirt road and continue to the light.

Point Aconi Light

This modern circular fiberglass tower with octagonal lantern is located on a point of land jutting sharply into the water. The name "Aconi" is thought to be from the Greek "acon", meaning "dart", the reference being to the pointed headland projecting into the sea.

Directions: From Trans Canada Hwy 105, take Route 162 and follow that road about 5mi. (8km). Turn right immediately before reaching the Point Aconi Generating Station and continue to a stop sign. Turn left; the road continues to the lightstation. (*See map location previous page*).

Sydney Front Range Light

Located on the south side of the North West Arm of Sydney Harbor, this octagonal wooden tower is not typical of most range light structures. The tower was built in 1905 and originally had a reflective light, now replaced with modern equipment. The rear light is across the road.

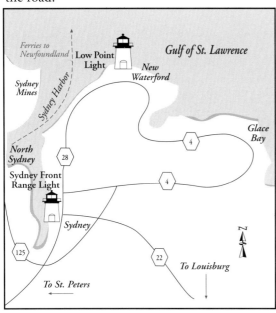

Directions: From Highway 125, take Exit 4 onto Route 239 to a stop sign. Continue to a second stop sign, turn left and follow this road along the edge of the North West Arm to a narrow dirt lane on the left. The front range is in a field at the beginning of the road. The rear light is visible from Route 239.

Low Point Light

Built in 1938, Low Point light offers elements associated with a "classic" lighthouse. The octagonal concrete tower stands 68 feet (20.8m) and is located in New Victoria on a high point of land overlooking a fishing area. An old-style circular iron lantern, the only one left in Nova Scotia, surrounds the rotating white light. *Map location, page 78*

Photos © Chris Mills

Directions: At the intersection of Highway 125 and Route 4, continue into Sydney to Victoria Rd. Turn onto Route 28 toward New Waterford. In New Victoria, turn onto Brown's Rd and continue for about 0.5 mi (.8km). Turn right, continue to a dirt road and follow it to a gate and the light.

Louisbourg Light

Near the southeast corner of Cape Breton, Louisbourg was the fortress from which the French planned to hold New France against the English. Dependence upon ships from France for supplies caused concern for safe passage into the harbor. Initially open bonfires were lit on the headlands to guide vessels; a navigational cross also marked the entrance. In 1727 plans were put forth to build a lighthouse but the formal decision was not taken until the spring of 1729 after one of the King's ships, *Le Profund,* met an untimely end in the harbor.

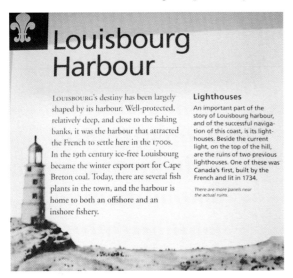

Louisbourg Harbour

LOUISBOURG's destiny has been largely shaped by its harbour. Well-protected, relatively deep, and close to the fishing banks, it was the harbour that attracted the French to settle here in the 1700s. In the 19th century ice-free Louisbourg became the winter export port for Cape Breton coal. Today, there are several fish plants in the town, and the harbour is home to both an offshore and an inshore fishery.

Lighthouses

An important part of the story of Louisbourg harbour, and of the successful navigation of this coast, is its lighthouses. Beside the current light, on the top of the hill, are the ruins of two previous lighthouses. One of these was Canada's first, built by the French and lit in 1734.

There are more panels near the actual ruins.

Construction of the lighthouse then began in 1731. The approximately 70-foot circular tower was made of coursed rubble and completed in 1733, the first established in Canada and second in North America. Because shipment of some 400 small lantern panes from France was delayed, the sperm oil lantern was first lit in April, 1734. Reportedly the light was visible for 18 nautical miles. A small tax was levied on vessels using the harbor; revenues covered construction, upkeep and lightkeeper's salary.

The lantern design was faulty, however, offering the wood no protection from high temperatures generated by the open-flame light. In September, 1736 a fire gutted the lantern; the stone tower survived. A coal-and-wood-burning light was quickly reestablished on top of the remaining tower. The reconstructed lantern included a larger reservoir, placed in a water jacket to dissipate heat, and wicks spaced further apart to reduce heat intensity. Six stone pillars, a vault-shaped brick roof covered with lead, vents fitted into each of the six faces, and a chimney all were added to prevent future fires. This new light was completed in July, 1738; reflectors were added in 1751 to focus the light from the lamp wicks.

Cannon shots during the second British siege of Louisbourg in 1758 inflicted heavy damage to the tower. The structure was declared beyond repair and left to disintegrate. During the 19th century, when an effort was undertaken by maritime officials to reduce the incidence of shipwrecks along the Atlantic coast, one of the new lighthouses built was at Louisbourg, completed in 1842. The 2-1/2 storey wooden building also served as keeper's residence; the structure was white with black, vertical stripes. In 1922 fire again destroyed the light at Louisbourg.

The present tower, a 55-foot (15m) white, octagonal concrete structure, was completed in 1923. Now part of the Fortress of Louisbourg National Historic Site, the remains of the foundation of the second lighthouse are still visible near the tower.

"On this site was erected by France in 1731, the first lighthouse tower constructed of fireproof material in North America. Near here the British erected batteries to silence the defensive works erected by France on the island opposite the entrance. In 1745 these batteries were commanded by Lt. Col. John Gorham; in 1758 by Brigadier General James Wolfe."

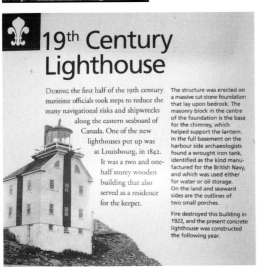

19th Century Lighthouse

DURING the first half of the 19th century maritime officials took steps to reduce the many navigational risks and shipwrecks along the eastern seaboard of Canada. One of the new lighthouses put up was at Louisbourg, in 1842. It was a two and one-half storey wooden building that also served as a residence for the keeper.

The structure was erected on a massive cut stone foundation that lay upon bedrock. The masonry block in the centre of the foundation is the base for the chimney, which helped support the lantern. In the full basement on the harbour side archaeologists found a wrought iron tank, identified as the kind manufactured for the British Navy, and which was used either for water or oil storage. On the land and seaward sides are the outlines of two small porches.

Fire destroyed this building in 1922, and the present concrete lighthouse was constructed the following year.

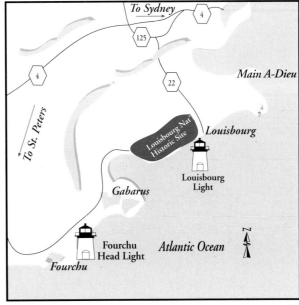

Directions: Take Route 22 into Louisburg; turn left onto Havenside Rd . Continue 3.5km (2.1mi) to Lighthouse Point and a parking area.

Fourchu Head Light

Fourchu Head is linked to the mainland village of Fourchu by a breakwater. The white circular fiberglass tower has two red horizontal bands with light showing fixed white. Originally built in 1907 with keeper's dwelling, the remains of foundations from those structures are still visible.

Directions: From Route 4 at St. Peters, turn south onto Route 247 and continue 8 mi. (13km). Turn left at the sign indicating Grand River and continue approximately 5.5 mi. (9km), turn right over the bridge and follow the sign to Fourchu. Continue approximately 24.5 mi. (39km), toward South Fourchu and onto a gravel road. Just past the wharfs there is a cemetery and the breakwater leading to the light. *Note map location, previous page.*

Grandique Point Light

Originally built in 1884, the standard "pepper shaker" style light overlooks Lennox Passage which separates Isle Madame from the mainland. The light is a fixed green beacon. The village of Martinique was founded by Acadians who unsuccessfully attempted to settle in the Caribbean then returned to Nova Scotia.

Directions: From Highway 104, take Exit 46 onto Route 320. Follow signs to Martinique (turn east) and continue to Lennox Passage Provincial Park and the light.

Marache Point Light

Marache Point Light

Grandique Point Light

Exhibiting a fixed white beam, this light was originally known as Arichat light. Established in 1851, it is a small pepper shaker structure which guides vessels into Arichat Harbor and marks the headland.

Directions: From Highway 104, take Exit 46 and continue to the junction with Routes 320 and 206. Follow Route 206 straight (signs to Arichat, the Petit-de-Grat). Turn west onto Lower Rd, turn left to Cape August (signs indicate). Continue to follow the directional signs to Cape August and Clearwater. Continue straight at the yield sign (do not turn left to Clearwater). Follow this road to a turnaround area; park or continue as passable to the light.

Jerome Point Light

This light was built in 1883 at Jerome Point to guide mariners into St. Peters Canal which separates the Bras d'Or Lake from the Atlantic Ocean. The tapered wooden tower shows a fixed red beam. Construction of the canal was undertaken in 1854 with renovations to its present size continuing until 1917.

Directions: In St. Peters, follow Route 4 across the Canal and turn into Battery Provincial Park. The lighthouse is across the road from the campground headquarters.

Refer to map shown below for location for Grandique and Marache Point lights, pictured on previous page. See page 77 for Kidston Island map location.

Kidston Island Light

The light is located on the northeast end of the island and is easily seen from the village of Baddeck, marking the harbor entry. A seasonal shuttle service runs to the island.

Directions: Take the exit to Baddeck from the TransCanada 105; the island is just off the harbor.

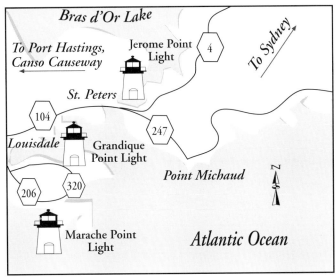

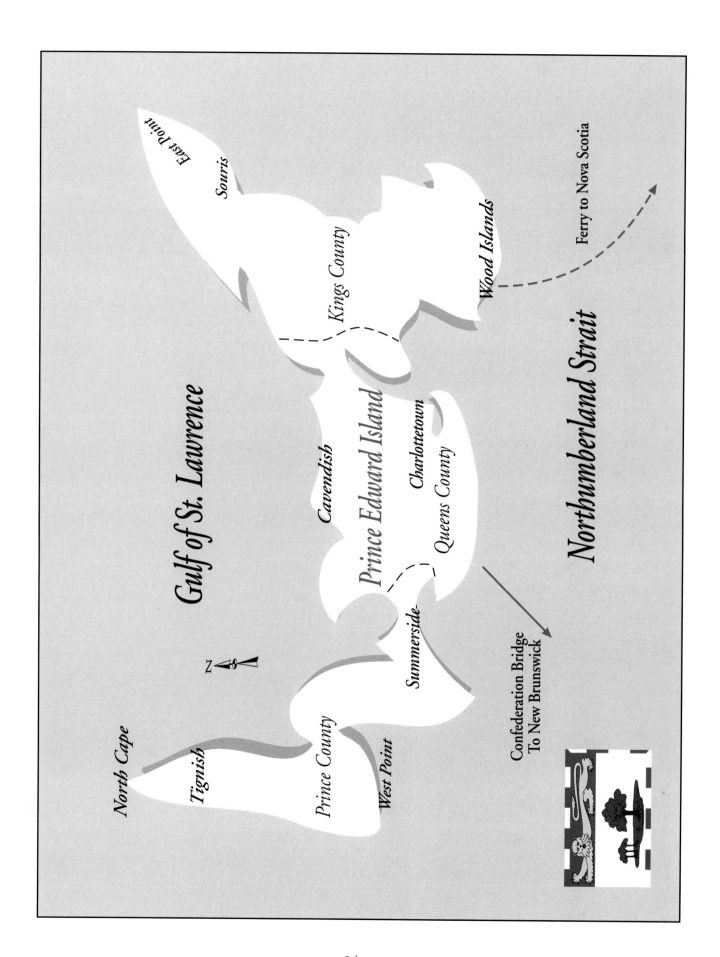

Gulf of St. Lawrence

North Cape

Tignish

Prince County

West Point

Summerside

Cavendish

Prince Edward Island

Charlottetown

Queens County

Kings County

Souris

East Point

Wood Islands

Ferry to Nova Scotia

Northumberland Strait

Confederation Bridge
To New Brunswick

N

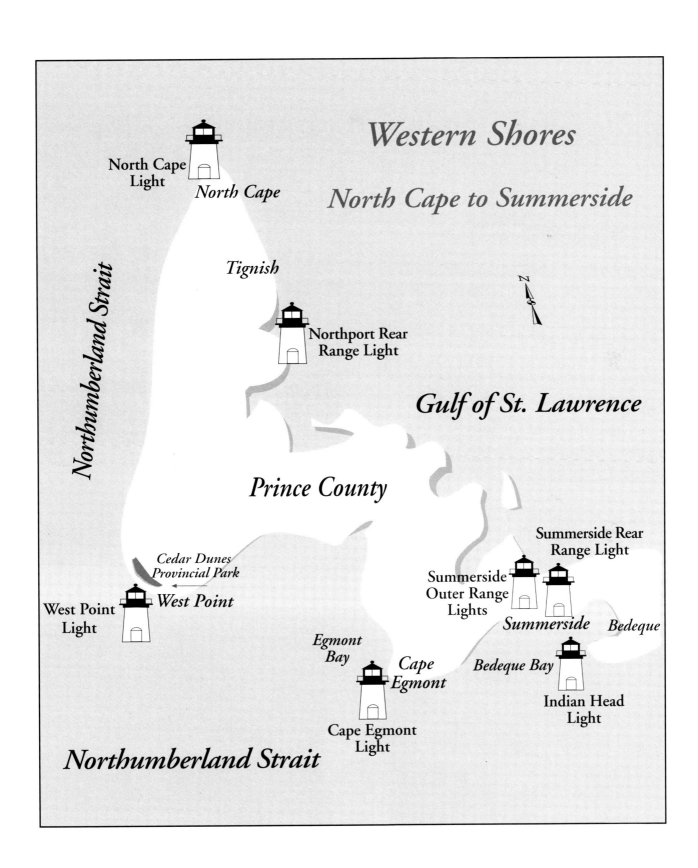

North Cape Light

North Cape

Western Shores

North Cape to Summerside

Tignish

Northport Rear Range Light

Northumberland Strait

Gulf of St. Lawrence

Prince County

Cedar Dunes Provincial Park

West Point Light — *West Point*

Summerside Rear Range Light

Summerside Outer Range Lights

Summerside *Bedeque*

Egmont Bay

Cape Egmont

Bedeque Bay

Indian Head Light

Cape Egmont Light

Northumberland Strait

West Point Light

Located on a windswept bluff overlooking the western entrance to the Northumberland Strait, at the southwestern tip of Prince Edward Island, West Point light was initially completed in 1876. At 68 feet (20.6m), the square

tower is one of the tallest on the island. Because it was the first lighthouse built by the government on Prince Edward Island, the transfer of responsibility for aids to navigation passed from the colonial government to the new federal Department of Marine. Coincident with that change was the design change from octagonal to square towers.

Construction of the original tower began in 1875 under the supervision of William McDonald who then became the first keeper; he remained in the position for 50 years. His successor, Bennie MacIsaac was keeper until the 1963 automation and conversion to electric light. The tower tapers from 29 feet (8.8m) square at the base to 12 feet (3.7m) square at the top platform. The broad black horizontal bands originally were red, but were repainted in 1915 to provide more contrast against the sunsets. The attached dwelling is a 1980s reconstruction of the original keeper's quarters and now operates as a bed and breakfast.

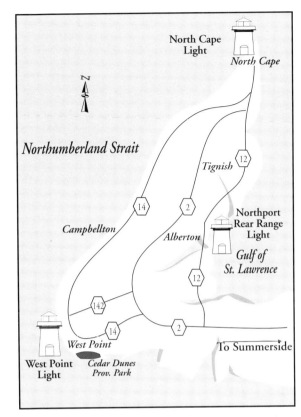

Directions: From Route 2, turn west onto Route 14 and continue into West Point. Follow the signs to Cedar Dunes Provincial Park. The light is to the right, just past the park entrance.

North Cape Light

A lighthouse has served fishermen and shipping interests at the northwestern point of Prince Edward Island since 1866. The first light was a portable lamp set up by local fishermen; the present structure was built in 1867. North Cape light warns mariners of the one-mile (1.5km) long natural rock reef that projects into the sea, one of the longest in the world.

Directions: Follow Route 12 to its end at North Cape. Or, Route 14 skirts the west shore of the island; a variety of crossroads (not all paved) will connect back to Route 12.

Northport Rear Range Light

This light is similar in design to the Summerside Rear Range light, but on a smaller scale. The front range light is a skeleton tower near the old railway wharf; both guide fishing vessels into the harbor.

Directions: Follow Route 12, turning off to Alberton; signs at the main intersection direct you to Northport. The light is to the left on the main road.

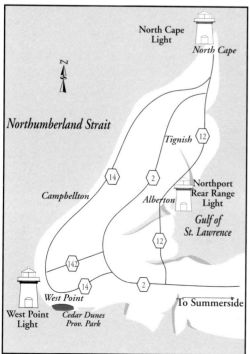

North Cape Light
North Cape

N

Northumberland Strait

Tignish 12

14

2

Campbellton

Alberton

Northport Rear Range Light

Gulf of St. Lawrence

12

142

14

2

West Point

To Summerside

West Point Light

Cedar Dunes Prov. Park

Summerside Range Lights

Rear Range Light

The western and southwestern shores of Prince Edward Island have a long history of shipbuilding, known for production of wooden sailing vessels. In the city of Summerside, homes can be seen which recall the prosperous Age of Sail during the 1800s.

Two sets of range lights guide vessels into the harbor. The Summerside Rear Range light is a 65-foot (20m) tall tapered tower; a skeleton tower near the outer edge of the wharf is the front range light. The Outer Range lights are located on the western edge of the city and are both of traditional pepper shaker design.

Directions: On the east side of the city on Water St. (Route 11), turn south onto Glovers Shore Rd. The **rear range** is on private property on the right side of the road. Continue on Route 11 to the west side of Summerside. Turn onto McKenzie Rd; the front range light is on the left. The rear range is on the main road.

Outer Range Light

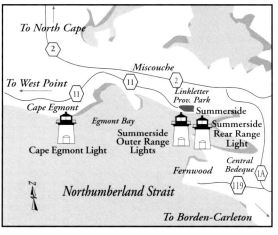

Cape Egmont Light

Vessels travelling through the Northumberland Strait have been guided past Egmont and Bedeque Bays by this light since it was first put into operation in 1884.

Directions: Follow Route 11 through Cap-Egmont village; turn onto the road to the wharf, then left onto a dirt road leading to the light.

Indian Head Light

Located at south entrance to Summerside Harbor, Indian Head light is a unique structure on the island at end of a one-mile-long breakwater off MacCallums Point. The light was built in 1881; the first keeper was Captain Charles Peters. At 40 feet (12m) tall, the octagonal tower is mounted atop a larger octagonal building intended to serve as keeper's quarters although no one has actually lived there. At low tide it is possible to walk across the breakwater and sandbar to the light; it is also distantly visible from Summerside waterfront.

Directions: In Bedeque at the intersection of Routes 171 and 112, continue on Route 112 to the end-- about 5.5 miles (9km). The pavement ends at about 3.5 mi (5.5km); the narrow dirt road continues to the point.

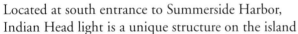

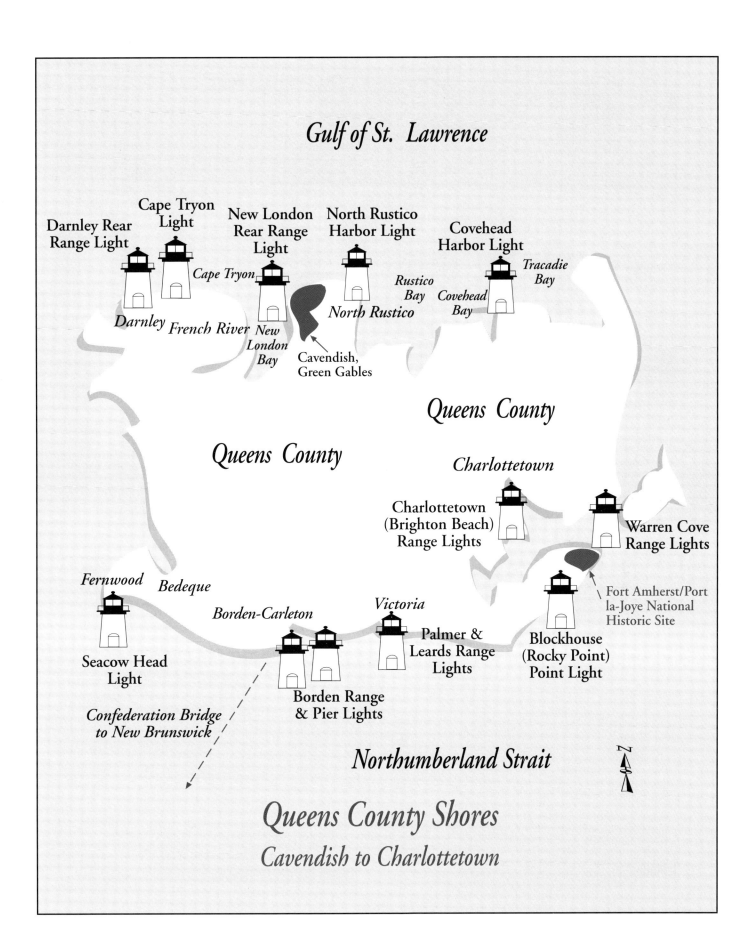

Gulf of St. Lawrence

Darnley Rear Range Light

Cape Tryon Light

New London Rear Range Light

North Rustico Harbor Light

Covehead Harbor Light

Cape Tryon

Rustico Bay

Tracadie Bay

Covehead Bay

Darnley

French River

New London Bay

North Rustico

Cavendish, Green Gables

Queens County

Queens County

Charlottetown

Charlottetown (Brighton Beach) Range Lights

Warren Cove Range Lights

Fernwood

Bedeque

Borden-Carleton

Victoria

Palmer & Leards Range Lights

Fort Amherst/Port la-Joye National Historic Site

Seacow Head Light

Blockhouse (Rocky Point) Point Light

Confederation Bridge to New Brunswick

Borden Range & Pier Lights

Northumberland Strait

N

Queens County Shores

Cavendish to Charlottetown

91

Port Borden Range Lights

Seacow Head Light

Established in 1863, the 60-foot (18m) octagonal tower overlooks the Northumberland Strait and Confederation Bridge. The structure has been moved back from its original location due to erosion.

Directions: On Route 119, follow signs to Fernwood. At the "T" intersection, turn left onto the dirt road to Seacow Head; the light is visible as you drive toward it.

The range lights were built in 1917 to guide mariners into Borden. Discontinuation of the ferry from New Brunswick has made the lights now unnecessary. The front light is being refurbished and will be part of the Gateway Village.

Port Borden Pier Light

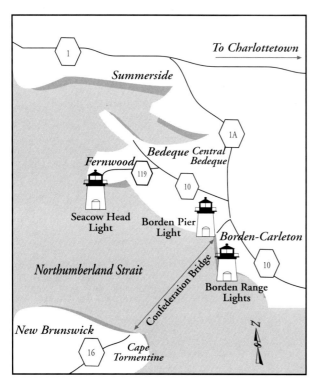

The lighthouse at the Port Borden pier was a guidepost for ferry traffic into Port Borden. With harbor traffic now greatly reduced, the light may soon be decommissioned.

Directions: Both the range light and pier light can be seen from Carlton St., just east of the Gateway Village in Borden-Carleton. The front range light is on the grounds of the Gateway Village.

Warren Cove Range Lights

Both lights are of standard pepper shaker style, located on the grounds of the Ft. Amherst/Port-la-Joye National Historic Site.

Directions: From Route 1 at Cornwall, follow Route 19 to the Fort Amhers/Port-la-Joye National Historic Site.

(Note map location(s), following page)

Leards & Palmer Range Lights

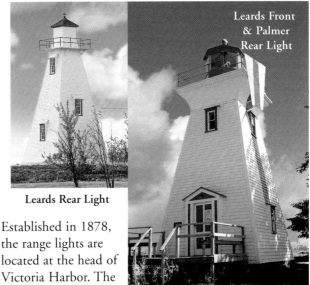

Leards Front & Palmer Rear Light

Leards Rear Light

Established in 1878, the range lights are located at the head of Victoria Harbor. The "double" tower now functions as the front light for Leards and rear light for Palmer Range lights, with two lights positioned in the lantern in separate directions. Often cited as among the oldest lights on the island, it also operates as the Victoria Seaport Museum. The Leards Rear light is on private property; the Palmer Front light is a skeleton structure.

Directions: The Leards rear light is visible on private property on Route 10; the "double" range light is in Victoria on Water St. at the head of the harbor.

Brighton Beach (Charlottetown) Range Lights

Although the front tower is of standard tapered design, the rear light, a modern "applecore" structure, is unique to PEI. Both are on private property but easily visible.

Directions: Follow signs to the waterfront/Victoria Park in Charlottetown.

93

Blockhouse
(Rocky Point) Light

Adjacent to Ft. Amherst/Port-la-Joye National Historic Park at the west side of the entrance to Charlottetown Harbor, the first light at this location was established in 1849. The present lighthouse and dwelling, the second oldest on Prince Edward Island, were built in 1876 and are still in use. This two-storey keeper's house is distinctive, as most were small attachments to the light tower or were separate structures. The original lantern was a kerosene lamp, later changed to gas lantern. When the station was automated in 1962, an electric mercury vapor light with increased range of 18 nautical miles was installed.

Directions: At Cornwall, turn off onto Route 19 west of Charlottetown and continue to the Fort Amherst/Port-la-Joye National Historic Site. Follow the dirt road straight rather than turning into the park; the light station is at the road's end.

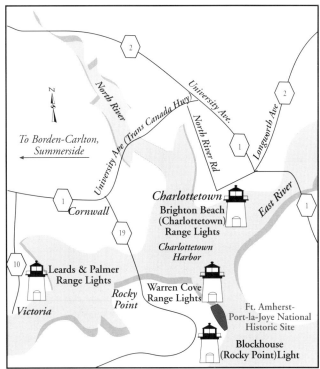

New London Rear Range Light

The rear range light on New London Bay, east of French River, was built 1876. During a severe gale in 1879, the lighthouse was lifted off its foundation and deposited 650 feet (198m) westward to the present location. Extensive renovations were undertaken in 1944. The flashing electric light still functions seasonally, but the dwelling has been leased since 1968 as a summer cottage.

Directions: From Route 20, turn north onto River Road and continue to Cape Rd. Turn right and continue to the end. The light is to the right with a dirt path/drive leading to it.

(*Map location, next page*)

North Rustico Harbor Light

Located on the North Shore at the entrance to North Rustico Harbor, a lighthouse was first established here in 1876. The present structure, built 1899, was renovated in 1921; the dwelling remains attached. In 1978 the wooden tower was raised four feet (1.2 meters) to increase the range of the light. The tower is 29 feet (8.8 meters) tall and tapers from 15.5 feet (4.7 meters) square at the base to seven feet (2.2 meters) at the top. The station was automated in 1960.

Directions: Turn off Route 6 at North Rustico and continue to North Rustico Harbor. The light is easily seen.

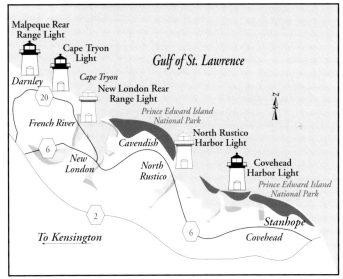

Cape Tryon Light

Located at the tip of Cape Tryon, the original tower and keeper's dwelling were relocated due to erosion. The present structure was built in 1905 and automated in 1962.

Malpeque Rear Range Light

This small pepper shaker light sits in the middle of a field adjacent to a private way but is visible from the main road. The front range is of the same size, located near the shoreline but also on private property

Directions: From Route 20 in Darnley, turn north on Profitts Point Rd. The rear range light is to the right.

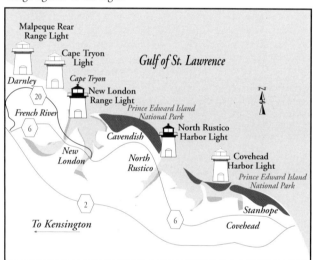

Directions: From Route 20 at French River, turn onto River Road, continue to Cape Road and turn left(a dirt/gravel road). Proceed approximately 0.6mi (1km); turn right onto a narrow dirt road and continue to its end and the light.

Covehead Harbor Light

The typical pepper-shaker style light is located in the dunes at Stanhope Cape in Prince Edward Island National Park. In 1851 the Yankee Gale took the lives of many American seamen; they are buried in a cemetery nearby and a plaque on the lighthouse commemorates their lives.

Directions: From Route 6 in Stanhope, follow the Gulf Shore Parkway, a paved road running parallel to the ocean. The light is on park grounds.

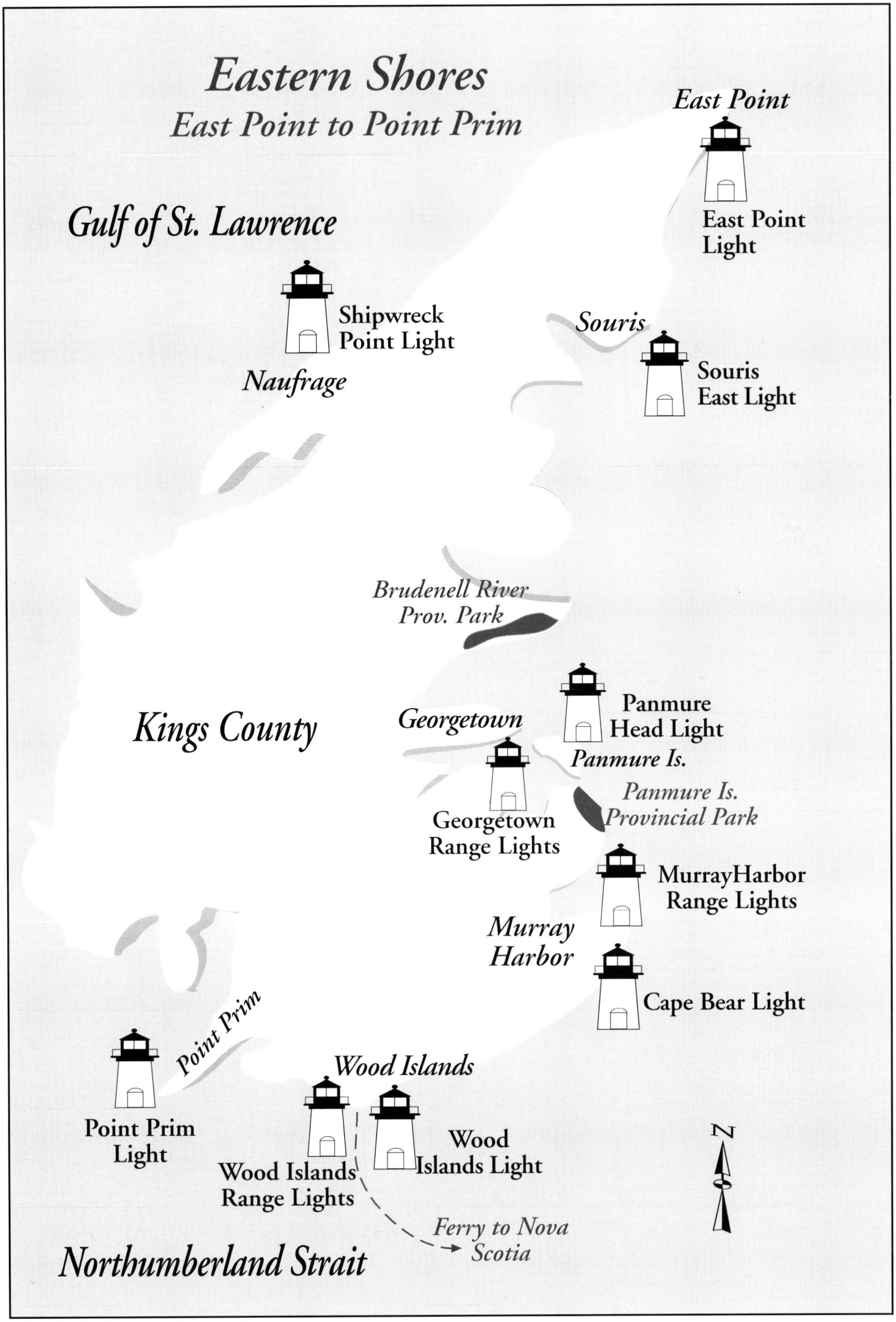

Eastern Shores
East Point to Point Prim

Gulf of St. Lawrence

East Point

East Point Light

Shipwreck Point Light

Naufrage

Souris

Souris East Light

Brudenell River Prov. Park

Kings County

Georgetown

Panmure Head Light

Panmure Is.

Panmure Is. Provincial Park

Georgetown Range Lights

Murray Harbor Range Lights

Murray Harbor

Cape Bear Light

Point Prim

Wood Islands

Point Prim Light

Wood Islands Range Lights

Wood Islands Light

→ *Ferry to Nova Scotia*

N

Northumberland Strait

Point Prim Light

Built 1845-47, the lighthouse at Point Prim was the first round, brick lighthouse in Canada. It is the oldest operational lighthouse on Prince Edward Island and one of the tallest on the island at 60 feet (18.3 meters). The tower stands on a point of land at the southern end of Hillsborough Bay on the outer approach to Charlottetown Harbor.

In 1845 the Prince Edward Island House of Assembly approved a grant for the construction of a lighthouse on a nine-acre (3.6 hectare) site donated by Lord Selkirk. The first keeper was William Finalyson. In winter local residents in sleighs would cross the ice from Charlottetown to inspect the completed building. The lighthouse was extensively renovated in 1884 but remains in original condition except for the veneer of shingles applied in the early 1900s. The present light is a mercury vapor lamp with a range of 20 nautical miles, the last of its kind to be installed on Prince Edward Island.

The light was automated in 1969; in 1976 the adjacent keeper's house was sold and removed. The tower is open during July and August.

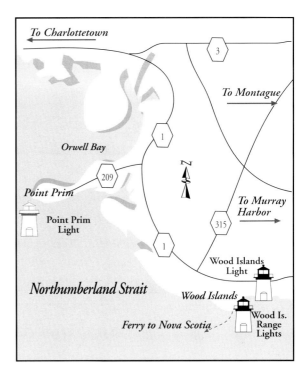

Directions: From the Trans-Canada Highway (Route 1) between Charlottetown and Woods Island, turn south onto Route 209 and follow the road to its end.

Wood Islands Light

Established in 1876, the square tower, 50 feet (15.2m) tall with attached dwelling, is located just east of the main entry to Wood Islands Harbor. Major renovations to the dwelling were completed in 1950. A hand-operated fog horn was installed at the harbor in 1941 but when the fog horn was automated in 1979, there was no longer need for an assistant keeper. The lighthouse was electrified in 1958 and fully automated in 1989, one of the last to be manned. The lighthouse now overlooks the ferry terminal at Wood Islands and is part of a Provincial Park. During the season the lighthouse operates as a museum. *(Map location following page)*

Directions: Follow the drive from the Visitor Information Center at the Wood Islands ferry terminal.

Wood Islands Range Lights

Established in 1902, these lights are located on the pier leading into the ferry terminal at Wood Islands. Vessels entering the harbor align the light from the higher rear range directly above the light of the front range light, indicating correct position when entering the channel.

Directions: The lights are at the pier, just past the Wood Islands light; follow the dirt road from the Visitors Information Center.

Cape Bear Light

Located on southeastern tip of Prince Edward Island, the lighthouse was established in 1881, a three-storey tower 39 feet (12m) tall, 76 feet (23 m) above the water. During World War II the lighthouse was useful in spotting German U-boats nearing the coast. Recent renovations have been completed and the tower is now open in season. *(Map location, following page)*

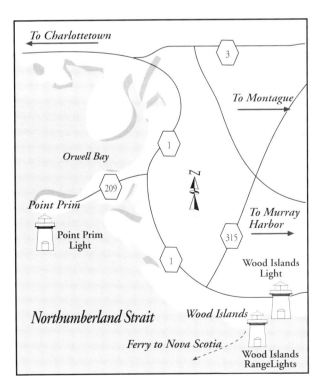

Directions: From Route 18 at Cape Bear, continue straight onto a dirt road(if approaching from the west)--or turn left onto the dirt road if approaching from the north. Turn right at the second dirt lane; the light is just ahead to the right.

Murray Harbor Range Lights

Rear Range Light

Front Range Light

These lights guide fishing vessels into Murray Harbor. The front range light is small and has an unusual grey lantern, whereas the rear light is of more typical style. On the beach at Oldstore Point, the front light is almost a mile distant from the rear beacon which is located on private property.

Directions: On Route 18 just east of the village of Murray Harbor, at Beach Point, turn onto Beach Rd.; continue to the light. To view the rear light, turn off Route 18 at Wharf Rd; the light is visible to the left located on private property.

Georgetown Rear Range Light

The rear range light is a pepper-shaker design, but much taller and more tapered than most of that style. Located on St. Andrews Point, the front range light is a modern, circular metal structure with open light and red and white horizontal bands. Although located on private property the rear tower is visible directly from the road.

Directions: Follow Route 17 from Montague about 6mi (10km); turn onto Lower Montague Rd. and continue as the road skirts the shore. The rear light is to the right, the front light at the point, visible across the road.

Panmure Head Light

The octagonal, freestanding 58 foot (17.7m) tower was built in 1853 to warn ships away from Bear Reef and Panmure Ledge. Major renovations to the structure were undertaken in 1861, 1875 and 1956. The light was electrified in 1958 and fully automated in 1985. Built in 1958, the lightkeeper's house is now privately owned. The tower is open during the season.   *(Map location, following page)*

Directions: From Route 17, take Route 347 across Panmure Island. The light is visible as you approach; turn right onto a dirt road to the light station.

Souris East Light

Established in 1880, the light at Souris guides local fishing vessels and ferry traffic to the Magdalen Islands. Located at the tip of Knight Point, southeast of the breakwater, this station was one of the last to be automated; it was destaffed in 1991. The lantern is of classic round metal style, not common to the lights of Prince Edward Island.

Directions: From Route 2/16 in Souris, turn onto MacPhee Avenue (signs direct you to Magdalen Islands/Isles de la Madeleine ferry). Turn left onto Breakwater St.; the light is on the right.

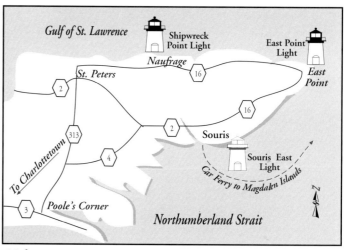

East Point Light

East Point Light now sits on point of land at the extreme eastern tip of the island although it was originally built (1867) on a higher piece of land 1/2 mile inland from the present location. The grounding of the British warship

Phoenix in 1882 was blamed on the fact the lighthouse was so far removed from the point. Consequently, in 1885 the lighthouse was relocated. At that time a fog alarm was installed in an adjacent building. Erosion of the nearby seaside cliffs required the lighthouse to again be relocated in 1908, this time 200 feet (61m) inland to the present location; a new fog alarm building was constructed on the former site of the tower.

The first keeper was Alexander Beaton, owner of the farm on which the lighthouse now stands. In 1867 the first keeper's house was built, with an addition in 1885. This dwelling was replaced in 1923, with

quarters for two assistants constructed in 1966 and 1972. The light, automated in 1989, has a range of 20 nautical miles.

East Point Light (con't)

Treasure hunters have sought to unearth some of Captain Kidd's bounty in the nearby woods west of the lighthouse. Legend suggests that, from the lighthouse, World War II German U-boats could be heard recharging their batteries in the Northumberland Strait. Cannonballs, deck plates and girders from wrecked ships have been found driven ashore by storms and a victim of one of the shipwrecks is buried nearby. The former keeper's house is now a gift shop.

Directions: Follow Route 16 to East Point; signs direct you to the light and park area.

Shipwreck Point Light

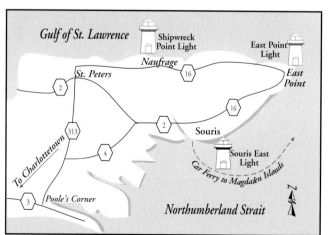

This octagonal tower, at 47 feet (14m), is located on the north shore of the island at Shipwreck Point. The occulting white light has a range of 18 nautical miles.

Directions: From Route 16 in Naufrage, follow the signs to Shipwreck Point. A path beside private property leads to the light.

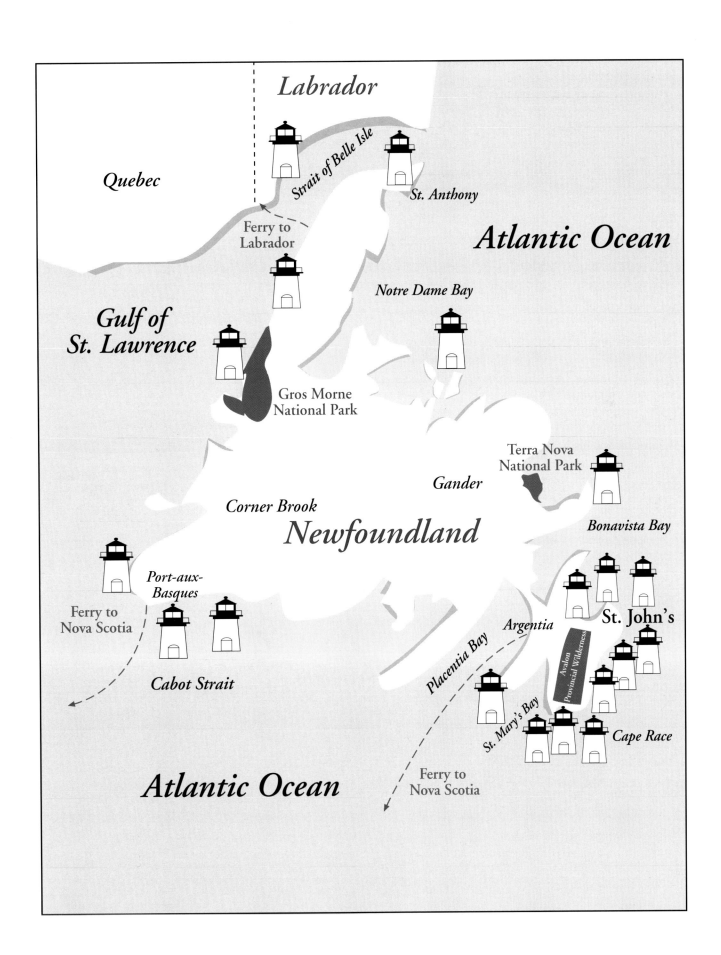

Labrador

Quebec

Strait of Belle Isle

St. Anthony

Atlantic Ocean

Ferry to Labrador

Notre Dame Bay

Gulf of St. Lawrence

Gros Morne National Park

Terra Nova National Park

Gander

Corner Brook

Newfoundland

Bonavista Bay

St. John's

Port-aux-Basques

Ferry to Nova Scotia

Argentia

Placentia Bay

Avalon Provincial Wilderness

Cabot Strait

St. Mary's Bay

Cape Race

Atlantic Ocean

Ferry to Nova Scotia

Cape Race Light

Vessels departing for the New World in the 19th and early 20th centuries set a course for Cape Race lighthouse. Located on the southeast coast of the Avalon Peninsula, this light was the first landfall for millions of European immigrants venturing to the New World, a new beginning and was the first land sited by most North Atlantic shipping to Canada. Jagged cliffs nearly 100 feet high mark this part of the coast which has been labelled one of the most frightening in the world, with fog, icebergs and storms--oftentimes all at once-- a threat to mariners. More than 300 shipwrecks have occurred in the area.

The 1856 iron tower was equipped with a fixed white catoptric light with 13 argand lamps and reflectors, visible from 180 feet above sea level to 17 nautical miles in clear weather. A wooden dwelling and covered walkway were built for the keeper. A tax levied on all trans-Atlantic shipping to and from the Gulf of St. Lawrence funded maintenance of the lightstation. This light, however, did not prevent further shipwrecks. On Christmas Day, 1856, the thick fog obliterated the light at 400 yards. The *Westford*, headed for Liverpool, struck the rocks below the lighthouse; only four survivors were rescued by the lightkeepers. Moreover, in 1863 thick fog caused the mail steamer *Anglo-Saxon* to go ashore near Cape Race, claiming 238 lives despite rescue efforts by the lightstation crew.

A "quick" passage to England from Newfoundland was offered aboard mailboats. After travelling from St. John's to Cape Race, passengers would find themselves atop a 100 foot cliff with a single iron ladder leading down to the pilot ship. After negotiating that initial treacherous trip, legend had it that the remainder of the voyage would be smooth sailing. Mail arriving for Newfoundland was "delivered" at Cape Race. In heavy seas, cannisters were tossed overboard; local fisherman passing by would collect the containers, present them to the local postmaster and receive five pounds sterling.

(See map location, page 112)

In 1866 the light was changed from fixed to revolving and a new lantern, lights and clockwork mechanism were installed. A steam whistle was added in 1872; a ten-second blast every minute warned vessels away from the cliffs in fog or snow-storms. Although the audible range was claimed to be 20 nautical miles in calm weather, that range was reduced to seven nautical miles against wind or storm.

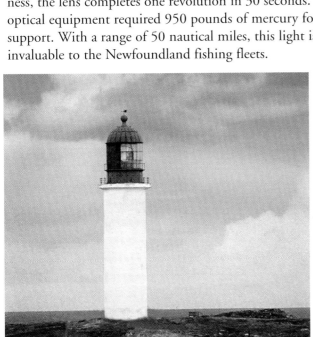

The original light tower was replaced in 1907 with a concrete structure, 18 feet in diameter and 96 feet tall. The lantern enclosing the lighting apparatus is the same diameter as the tower, weighs 24 tons and contains a seven-ton, 12-foot tall hyper-radial lens. This lens, the largest type built, consists of thousands of reflecting prisms and projecting lenses each with four optical faces, each more than eight feet in diameter. Floating in a mercury bath to get the right speed and steadi-ness, the lens completes one revolution in 30 seconds. This optical equipment required 950 pounds of mercury for support. With a range of 50 nautical miles, this light is a major beacon for North Atlantic shipping and is also invaluable to the Newfoundland fishing fleets.

The Coast Guard has agreed to turn over the outbuild-ings to the local historical society for preservation and restoration as an interpretive center. The group plans to restore the assistant keepers house as a visitor informa-tion center; the wireless station, which received the last Titanic transmission and news of its sinking, also will be restored.

"Built in 1907 by the Canadian Government, this lighthouse on the approaches to the nation's busiest shipping lane, replaced an earlier one erected by the imperial government in 1856 on the same site. Its overall height of 96 feet comprises a circular stone and concrete tower 68 feet high surmounted by a lantern over 17 feet in diameter. The lantern originally housed a petroleum vapor light rotated by a clockwork mechanism on a mercury float. The massive optic, made by Chance Brothers of Birmingham, emitted a flash of over 1,000,000 candle power. The light was electrified in 1926."

Directions: From Route 10 at Portugal Cove South, turn east onto the unpaved road--a sign indicates Cape Race 12 miles (20km). The lighthouse is at the end of the road.

Cape Pine Light

Although by the mid 1800s five lighthouses had been built in Newfoundland, they were all on the east coast; the treacherous Avalon south coast had none. Numerous British warships had been claimed by these waters, along

with tragic loss of life. Finally, the English government in 1851 began construction of a lighthouse at Cape Pine, the southernmost tip of Newfoundland.

Designed in England, the tower was a cast iron structure with ornate circular stairway in the 45-foot tower. The choice of cast iron, the new building material of the 19th century, was intended to meet demands of budget, ease of construction and durability. Initially no keeper's dwelling was

built; it was assumed the tower would be sufficient lodging. However, the keepers quickly abandoned that notion during the first winter, choosing to live in the shed previously used by workmen. A separate wooden keeper's house was built the following summer, along with a 13-mile road to the nearest community, Trepassey. The light is now automated and was destaffed in 1996.

Directions: Follow Route 90 and/or Route 10 to Trepassey, turn at the sign indicating St. Shotts. Bear left onto a gravel road at a small sign indicating historic site and continue to the lighthouse.

Powles Head Light

Marking the outer entrance to Trepassey Harbor, Powles Head light is one of the 24 remaining staffed light stations in Newfoundland. Established in 1902, the lantern contains a fourth order lens. The structure is of the typical utilitarian style, with a square tower attached at the corner of a small square building.

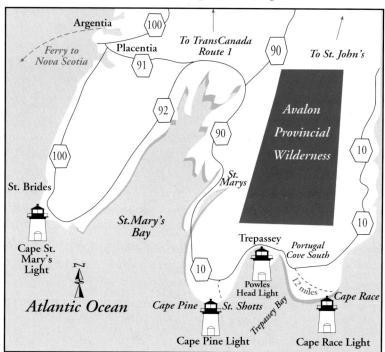

Directions: From the TransCanada Hwy, follow Route 90 through Peter's River; the road becomes Route 10. Or follow Route 10 along the southeastern shore. In Trepassey, turn onto Trepassey Rd and continue to the lighthouse.

In 1621, a colony was established on the Eastern shore of the Avalon peninsula by Lord Baltimore, Secretary of State for King James I. His stay was short lived. Finding the weather not to his liking, Lord Baltimore departed two years later, founding the Colony of Maryland and the City of Baltimore. The remains of that first settlement are today being unearthed by archaeologists.

The lighthouse at Ferryland Head was built in 1871 at the tip of a long, narrow point of land. Although the circular tower looks like a number of other Newfoundland light towers, in this case the main tower is made of brick, coated with steel on the outside to protect against fire and weather. A keeper's house also was built at the same time. Ice storms were a frequent occurrence and provided insulation against the fierce, chilling winds. The station is now automated.

Ferryland Head Light

Directions: From Route 10 along the eastern coast of the Avalon Peninsula, turn at Ferryland and follow the signs to the archaeological dig and interpretive center. A sign indicates the narrow road bearing right to the lighthouse. Cars must bear right at a small turn out; the light is about 1/2 mile walk from there.

Bull Head Light

Established in 1908, the light looks out onto Witless Bay which is the nesting site of puffins, and other seabirds.

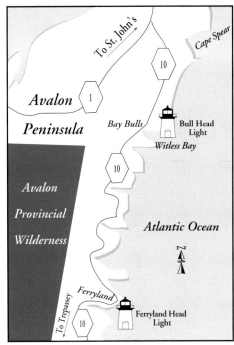

Directions: From Route 10 on the east Avalon coast, turn at Bay Bulls toward the harbor. Getting to the lighthouse requires a 2.5 mile hike along the East Coast Trail. Follow the road along the north side of the harbor to its end and the trail head.

Cape Spear Light

Cape Spear is a headland which runs into the sea 20 miles east of St. John's; the New World is closest to the Old at this point of land. As the most easterly point in North America, the cape was the site for construction in 1835 of Newfoundland's second lighthouse, marking the outer bay of St. John's. The original stone tower was built at the center of a classically styled keeper's house located atop a 300-foot sandstone cliff ; the tower then anchored the house to the rock.

In July, 1835 the frigate *Rhine* was trapped in thick fog near St. John's harbor. The captain of the boat that guided the vessel through the narrows was James Cantwell. On board the frigate was Prince Henry of the Netherlands who, in gratitude for safe passage, later granted Cantwell his request to become keeper of Cape Spear light, then under construction. The post was passed on to his descendents, with seven generations of Cantwells tending lights at Cape Spear.

The original light consisted of seven reflector lights brought from Scotland especially for this lighthouse. Atop the lighthouse at 246 feet above the sea, the lights could be seen for 18 nautical miles. Replaced by the current concrete structure in 1955, the original lighthouse is now part of a National Historic Park opened in 1983. The station was destaffed in 1996.

Directions: In St. John's, follow Water St. to Leslie St; turn south, crossing the bridge. At the intersection continue straight ahead 6.5 miles (11km) on Cape Spear Drive (Route 11) to the historic site and the lighthouse. *See map, following page.*

Fort Amherst Light

In 1813 Newfoundland's first navigational light was placed atop a stone fortress known as Fort Amherst which guarded the entrance to St. John's harbor. The Narrows, a one-half mile channel separating the large inner harbor from the open North Atlantic, was difficult for mariners to negotiate, making the lighthouse a welcome addition. The original tower was replaced in 1852; the current wooden tower replaced that structure in 1952.

Directions: In St. John's follow Water St. to Leslie St.; turn south, then left at the intersection. Signs direct you to Ft. Amherst.

Cape St. Mary's Light

Built in 1858-60 to mark to entrance to St. Mary's and Placentia Bays, the lighthouse is located at the edge of steep cliffs in Eastern Canada's largest bird sanctuary. The nearby old garrison town of Placentia (originally Plaisance) was the base for French attacks pressed up and down the English Shore. Plaisance was the French colonial capital and was to have been the French gateway to the New World.

Directions: From Route 100 or Route 92 on the west Avalon peninsula, follow signs to Cape St. Mary's Ecological Reserve. The lighthouse is at the tip of the cape on the grounds of the reserve. ***See map location, page 112***

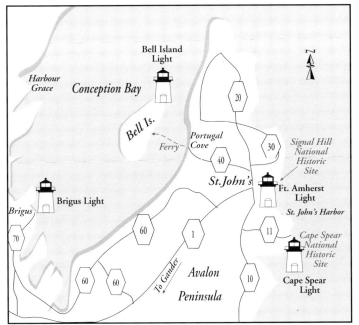

Bell Island Light

Just off the St. John's coast in Conception Bay, Bell Island light is a relatively new structure. The island was once home to one of the continent's most important iron ore mines, with shafts deep under the waters of the bay. Prior to 1940, iron ore carriers entering or leaving the bay had no guidance. The lighthouse and fog horn, built on the northeastern end of the island, were intended to aid these vessels. The lightstation is still staffed.

Directions: From Portugal Cove (just outside St. John's), the ferry to Bell Is. operates several times daily; the crossing takes 20 minutes. On Bell Is., there is a map of the island at the top of the road from the ferry. Bear left up the hill on "Main St". Turn right on East End Rd, continue to Lighthouse Rd which leads to the light station. *See map location, page 115.*

Brigus Light

Tracing its history back to 1612, Brigus was named after "Brickhouse", an old town in England. In the late 1700s Brigus was the most progressive and prosperous settlement in Conception Bay. The 19th century saw the area become a major sealing port and a light was established in 1885. The attached keeper's house was torn down in the 1930s but the iron tower is the original.

See map location, Page 115

Directions: From the TransCanada Hwy, take Route 70 to Brigus. Follow the Conception Bay Hwy to Brigus and Station Rd; continue to North St, bearing to the right to Harbor Drive. Park at the end of the road, where the trail to the lighthouse begins. It is about an hour's walk to the light.

Cape Bonavista Light

Europeans first visited the headland known as Cape Bonavista in 1497; John Cabot claimed this point of land ("New Founde Lande") for King Henry VII of England five years after Columbus discovered the West Indies.

Some 350 years later, with the development of the Labrador fishery and the sealing industry in the mid 1800s, there was a growing need for lighthouses on the northeast coast of Newfoundland.

Bonavista was a busy fishing community in the 1830s, with a population of 1500. An entirely seafaring town, the people relied on the water for a living and a link to the rest of the colony and the world. In 1841 the government of Newfoundland authorized construction of a stone lighthouse on the well-known headland on the coast marking the entrances of Trinity and Bonavista Bays. Construction commenced immediately; the building was completed in 1843 and the light put into operation in September, 1843.

The original lighthouse, designed by Trinity House in England, was a square, two storey wooden structure built around the circular stone tower which rose through the center of the building and supported the lantern. The structure was similar to those at Cape Spear (1836) and Harbour Grace Island (1837).

A revolving red and white catoptric (reflecting) light was removed from Bell Rock Lighthouse in Scotland and installed at Cape Bonavista. Each of the sixteen argand burners was centered inside a curved reflector. The burners and reflectors were mounted on a metal frame which revolved at regulated intervals powered by a weight-driven clockwork mechanism. Every two hours the mechanism had to be rewound. In 1895, this apparatus was replaced by another catoptric light (originally in service at the Isle of May lighthouse in Scotland) with six argand burners and reflectors, showing two white flashes, followed by one red flash. Polishing the reflectors was a three hour task. This apparatus was removed in 1962 and an electric light installed; four years later that light was placed on a metal tower. The 1895 catoptric light was then returned to the lighthouse, where it remains today; in total the light mechanism was in service for 84 years on both sides of the Atlantic.

For a time two families shared the living space at the lightstation; in 1855 a separate keeper's residence was built, with the assistant keeper and his family continuing to live in the lighthouse. About the same time a road was built, linking the lighthouse and the town of Bonavista, making isolation less of a problem for keepers and families. In the 1920s the keeper's residence was replaced by a one storey dwelling. A fog horn was installed in 1913 and had its own attendant operator until 1923. At that time the lightkeeper assumed those duties.

Cape Bonavista Light (con't)

The original lighthouse was transferred to the government of Newfoundland in 1970 for development as a Provincial Historic Site. The keeper's living quarters have been restored and furnished as they would have appeared in 1870. An interpretive center is located adjacent to the lighthouse. The Ryan Premises National Historic Site, a fully restored large-scale outport mercantile complex, is nearby; the site depicts the area's rich history of cod fishery.

Directions: From the TransCanada Hwy take the exit to Route 230 and Cape Bonavista. The route is well marked; follow it into the town of Bonavista. The lighthouse is about 2.5 miles (5Km) from the center of town; signs direct you to the site.

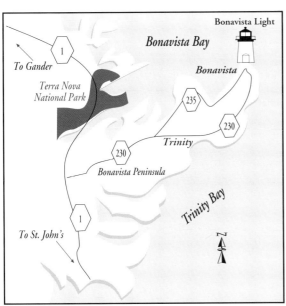

Long Point Light

Located 331 feet above sea level atop the cliff called Devil's Cove Head in Notre Dame Bay, Long Point light was built in 1875 of stone. The tower itself is only 47 feet tall. The original station had a duplex keeper's house but families of the lightkeepers would move off the island in winter as weather made travel back and forth impossible at times. Winds of 100mph are not uncommon here. Therefore, an enclosed walkway was built connecting the keeper's house, fog horn building and light tower. An aerobeacon-style lens replaced the original optic in the 1950s; the present light has a range of 22 nautical miles.

Twillingate Island is located in Notre Dame Bay and was given its name by French fishermen who thought the islands similar to a group of islands off the French coast called Toulinquet. History suggests the town was used as a fishing

port during the 15th and 16th centuries, but was without permanent settlement until the 18th century. By the winter of 1739, 152 people lived in Twillingate--English fishermen and their families from England. One of the province's oldest seaports, the population grew rapidly in the 18th century as a thriving fishing community prospered.

The northern provincial capital was located at Twillingate and, for 200 years, the town was the center of trade for Labrador and shore fisheries. However, implementation of the cod moratorium in the 1990s has now greatly reduced the local fishing industry.

Long Point Light (con't)

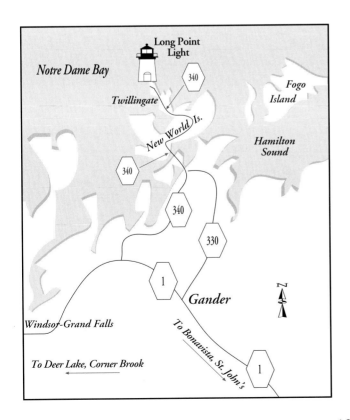

Directions: From the TransCanada, turn onto Route 340 to Lewisporte. Continue on Route 340 to New World Island, then Twillingate Island; the lighthouse is at the road's end. From Gander, turn onto Route 330, then 331 to 340 and the Isles.

Cape Norman Light

L'Anse aux Meadows is a tiny cove at the northernmost tip of Newfoundland. It is here that, in 980 A.D., Leif Ericson is said to have led a band of Greenland Vikings to the New World. Archaeologists have unearthed evidence of a Norse village at this site, which is now a Provincial Park. A lighthouse was built on the ragged cliffs of nearby Cape Norman in 1880 to mark the southern entrance to the Straits of Belle Isle. This area is one of the most treacherous in world, but with shipping lanes which must be negotiated to gain access to the Gulf of St. Lawrence.

Ironically, exotic arctic orchids are found in the limestone depressions that dot the rugged shoreline here, one of the few places in the world they can be seen despite the harsh conditions.

Directions: From Route 430, turn north to Cooks Harbor and Cape Norman. Bear left to Cape Norman; small signs direct you to the lighthouse. *Map location, following page.*

Point Riche Light

The original tower at Point Riche was built in 1871; the 1892 replacement structure still stands with a circular, traditional red lantern of classic style. Fire destroyed the keeper's house in the late 1970s. Near the lighthouse is an ongoing archaeological dig; investigators are searching for evidence of dwellings and artifacts from the 18th and 19th century French settlement at Port au Choix. In 1967, the Maritime Archaic Indian Burial Site excavated here held remains of 90 inhabitants and thousands of artifacts; the site is 3,200 to 4,200 years old. An interpretive center displays the findings and today the area boasts rich shrimp fishery.

Directions: From the TransCanada, take Route 430 through Gros Morne National Park and continue to Port au Choix. Turn east and follow signs to the National Historic Site. The lighthouse is at the end of that road.

See map location, page 124

Point Amour Light

Marking the northern entrance to the Straits of Belle Isle, this light was built by the government of Quebec in 1854-1857. At 109 feet, Point Amour light is the tallest in Atlantic Canada, second highest in all Canada. The

limestone tower was completed in 1857 and put into service the following year. An attached keeper's house also was built at that time. Several outbuildings were later added to the station: an oil shed in 1875, fog alarm building in 1907 (now demolished) and additional dwellings in 1954 and 1967. A second order Fresnel lens projects a beam visible for 18.5 nautical miles.

The shorter shipping route from Montreal and Quebec to the United Kingdom through the Straits of Belle Isle saves time, and therefore expense, versus the longer route via the Cabot Strait. However, ice and narrow passage prevented sailing vessels from using the straits to a significant extent. With the advent of steamships in the mid 1800s, this route gained popularity and four major lighthouses were designed and built. The construction of Point Amour was a three-year venture; supplies were landed from schooners at L'Anse au Loup, four miles distant from the lighthouse site. Stone quarries were opened, roads built and timber, shingle, brick and cut stone shipped from Quebec.

Numerous ships have been wrecked in the area. In 1855 two British warships broke up on the nearby rocks and in 1889 the *HMS Lily* sank. The lightkeeper saved several crewmembers from that vessel. Most recently, in 1922, the *HMS Raleigh,* flagship of the British North American Squadron, went aground in dense fog. Remains of the battleship are still scattered along the shore below the lighthouse.

In 1996 Point Amour light was automated and destaffed. The station now operates as a museum and Provincial Historic Site.

Directions: From the ferry landing at Blanc Sablon, turn east on Route 510. Follow signs to Point Amour and the light; the area is a Provincial Historic Site.

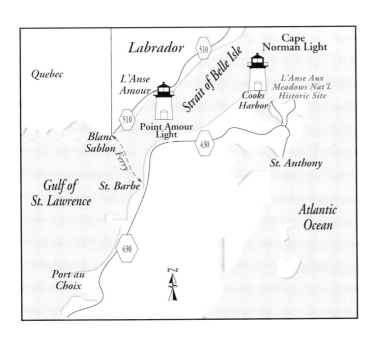

Lobster Cove Head Light

When the first lighthouses were built on the shores of Newfoundland, construction was difficult because no heavy equipment necessary to level the sites was available on the island. The original tower was built in 1871 and replaced with the current structure in 1892. Built in 1897, the keeper's house at Lobster Cove Head was built on several levels in order to conform to the rocky shore. The light was automated in 1970. The keeper's house is now an interpretive center for the Rocky Harbor area.

Directions: From the TransCanada Hwy, take Route 430 to Gros Morne National Park and Rocky Harbor. Follow the main road to the village and the lighthouse; signs direct you and the light is visible from the road at a distance.

Cape Ray Light

Located at one of the westernmost points in Newfoundland, the first lighthouse at Cape Ray was built in 1871; the original tower was replaced in 1885 after being destroyed by fire. That tower then burned in 1959 and was replaced with the present concrete structure. The area is now the site of an ongoing archaeological dig, the summer home of the Dorset Eskimos. The keeper's house is now a craft shop.

Note map location, page 126

Directions: From the ferry terminal in Port-aux-Basques, follow the TransCanada Hwy north for approximately 9 miles (15km). Turn west onto the Cape Ray access road and continue to its end and the light.

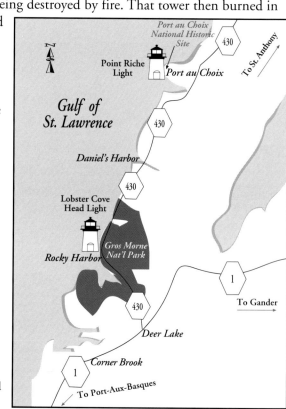

Rose Blanche Light (Restoration)

The Old Rose Blanche lighthouse is the last remaining granite lighthouse in Newfoundland. In 1871 Prescott Emerson presented a petition to the House of Assembly for Newfoundland for a lighthouse in his district; Rose Blanche Point was selected as the site. Built in 1873, the original structure was painted with red and white vertical stripes to offer a clear daymark against the grey stone, snow and ice. Locally quarried stone was used for construction of the tower and attached keeper's dwelling. The lighting apparatus, a fourth-order dioptric, was supplied by a Scottish engineering concern. At 95 feet above sea level, the fixed white beam was visible for 13 nautical miles in clear weather. In the 1940s the light was discontinued and moved to a nearby wooden, then later steel skeleton structure.

The dwelling and tower fell victim to vandalism and harsh weather conditions; by 1997 little remained of the original structure and the government wanted to demolish it entirely. However, a group of local residents worked with the Southwest Coast Development Association and began

ambitious efforts to rebuild the structure. Work began in the fall of 1997 to restore the exterior, then interior, of the lighthouse to its original condition.

Ninety percent of the original stones were recovered and reused. That work is now complete. The interior has been renovated and furnished as it was when a lightkeeper was in residence. A sixth order 1883 Fresnel lens is also on display.

Directions: From the ferry terminal at Port aux Basques, turn east and follow the signs to Rose Blanche. The route to the lighthouse is well marked.

Port-aux-Basques Light

Built in 1875, the circular iron tower is today the first lighthouse seen by visitors coming to Newfoundland by ferry from Nova Scotia. The station sits on a small island just off the Port-aux-Basques shore.

Directions: The light is visible from the ferry and from various points along the village coastline. It is just off the coast of the island.

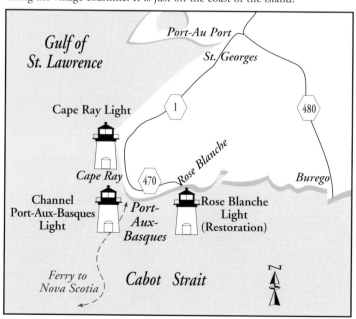

Index